ALMOST EVERYTHING YOU'VE EVER WANTED TO KNOW ABOUT

BASEBALL

Craig Nettles of the Yankees has hit more home runs than any other third baseman in Yankees' history—134.

ALMOST EVERYTHING YOU'VE EVER WANTED TO KNOW ABOUT
BASEBALL

DOM FORKER

Pagurian Press

DUTTON

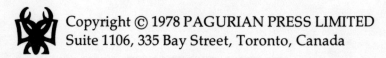
Library of Congress Catalog Card Number 78-18123
ISBN 0-525-03003-4
Printed and bound in Canada

*To my sons, Timmy, Geoffrey, and Teddy,
my numbers one, two, and three hitters;
and to my wife, Nancy, my clean-up batter.*

Johnny Allen of the Indians in a spectacular pitching position. Going into the last game of the 1937 season, he had a perfect 15 −0 record.

CONTENTS

The great Joe DiMaggio and his Yankee teammate Tommy Henrich in 1937, at the start of DiMaggio's big-time career.

INTRODUCTION

How does a boy of five acquire a love for baseball that will last for the rest of his life?

In my case it was easy. I chose the right hero—Joe DiMaggio. In retrospect, it seems as though he never disappointed me. Nor did the New York Yankees, as long as "The Yankee Clipper" glided, with gifted grace, across the center fields of my impressionable youth.

When I was five "Joltin' Joe" hit safely in 56 consecutive games. I can't remember the streak per se, but I do remember the words from a popular song that his streak inspired:

> He started baseball's famous streak,
> That's got us all aglow,
> He's just a man and not a freak—
> Joltin' Joe DiMaggio.
> . . . Coast to coast that's all you hear
> Of Joe the one-man show,
> He's glorified the horsehide sphere—
> Joltin' Joe DiMaggio.

The Joe DiMaggio feat that I cherish the most, however, was the one-man show he put on in Boston, midway through the 1949 season. [He had missed the first 65 games because of a painful heel that did not respond positively to an operation on a bone spur the previous winter.]

9

The Yankees got away from the plate quickly in 1949. But towards the end of June, the Boston Red Sox, the pre-season favorites, got hot and quickly closed the gap. Yankee fans feared the Red Sox would overtake the Pinstripers by July Fourth, long before Joe D. was due back in the line-up.

On June 29 the slumping Yankees travelled to Boston for a three-game weekend series against the Red Sox, who had reeled off nine victories in their last ten games. Allie Reynolds of the Yankees and Mickey McDermott of the Red Sox drew the starting assignments for the crucial first game. The 36,288 fans who jammed into Fenway Park on that evening got an unexpected treat when the public address announcer read aloud the starting line-ups. So did a 13-year-old boy in Bayonne, N.J., who leaned closer to the radio as Yankee announcer Mel Allen mellifluously addressed his audience: "In center field, for New York, batting fourth, number five, Joe DiMaggio . . . "

My first response was one of utter disbelief, which gave way to ecstatic jubilation. Then the sudden dawning of reality produced a sensation of uncertain dread. McDermott was young and strong, the fastest left-handed pitcher in the American League. DiMaggio was old and weak from prolonged idleness. His reflexes were bound to be slow. Could he get his still-powerful bat around on McDermott's quick serves, I wondered.

In the top of the second inning I found out. DiMaggio, swinging late, lifted two consecutive foul pops just beyond first baseman Billy Goodman's reach that landed in the box seats. But before my accelerating skepticism entirely enveloped me, Mel Allen's voice boomed over the radio, "DiMaggio lines a single over (Vern) Stephen's head into left center field. How about that!"

My father, a one-time Babe Ruth fan whose interest in baseball dropped off as the Yankees' success story multiplied— "Let somebody else win the pennant," he would say—smiled at me from his kitchen chair. My brother, a Stan Musial fan, exited from the room with a frown. In the same inning Hank Bauer homered with DiMaggio and Johnny Lindell on base to give the Yankees a 3-0 lead.

The following inning, DiMaggio came up with Phil Rizzuto on base. My brother, bound for an evening appointment, held the kitchen door half open, one foot on each side of the threshold, waiting to see what Joe D. would do. He didn't have to wait long. DiMaggio jumped on a McDermott fastball and put it into the screen for a two-run homer. I leaped into the air with unrestrained joy. Over the ecstatic voice of Mel Allen, I barely heard the slam of a door behind me. The Yankees went on to win the game, 5-4.

The next day the Yankees fell behind, 7-1. But DiMaggio, his old self again, greeted Ellis Kinder's fifth-inning serve with a three-run homer that narrowed the gap to 7-4. The inspired Yankees rallied to tie the score, 7-7, at the end of seven. In the top of the eighth, with two outs and no one on base, lefty Earl Johnson reached back for something extra. But DiMaggio, who was waiting at the plate, got all of the pitch, homering deep into the street in left for the deciding run in a 9-7 contest.

When DiMaggio started for his position in the bottom of the eighth, veteran shortstop Phil Rizzuto caught up to him and did something that the staid Yankees were not noted for. He grabbed his team leader's hand and danced all the way out to shortstop.

But DiMaggio's stirring performance was affecting not only his Yankee teammates and his fans, it also struck a sympathetic chord in the hearts of baseball fans all over the country. It was 1941 all over again. Could DiMaggio continue his unbelievable feats for one more game? If he could, the Red Sox' chances of catching the Yankees would be remote.

Two 20-game winners hooked up in the final game of the three-game set: Vic Raschi of the Yankees and Mel Parnell of the Red Sox. At the end of six innings, Raschi clung tenaciously to a 3-2 lead. In the top of the seventh, George Stirnweiss and Tommy Henrich each hit singles before "The Jolter" stepped into the box. Fenway Park was ominously silent. The count ran to three and two. Parnell deliberately moved into his stretch, reached back, and fired. DiMaggio waited . . . waited . . . waited and then with his uncanny last-second flick of the bat crashed a towering fly ball that landed in the left field light tower, high above "The Green Monster." He had saved his mightiest blow till last. And once again DiMaggio's blow proved to be the decisive one; this time in a 6-3 victory.

Overall, DiMaggio collected five hits in 11 at-bats, and he drove home nine runs, all clutch runs.

The stunned Red Sox did not quit in their race for the pennant though. They closed fast on the Yankees at the finish line; but the Bronx Bombers, pumped up by DiMaggio's .346 season, held on and won the pennant by one game.

How about that?

Since that memorable weekend I've always admired Herculean feats on the baseball diamond. When DiMaggio retired two years later, I learned to view the game more objectively. Gradually I began to truly appreciate the outstanding performances of unique players, past and present. In the meantime, I continued to root for the Yankees.

The more I've studied the game, the more I've been intrigued by it. Baseball is a funny game, Joe Garagiola once said. He was right. I always look for the expected, as baseball is a game of patterns, but I'm never surprised when I find the unexpected — it's a game of exceptions, too.

There are 1,001 facts, questions, and answers about North America's favorite game on the following pages. If you love baseball, the way I do, you're going to enjoy them.

THE HITTERS

Baseball Greats without a Home

No matter how great the player, he is rarely considered great enough in his owner's estimation. Quite often the owner will either trade or sell his star in an attempt to either get a better product or make a profit.

Take the all-time baseball team, for example.

Most baseball aficionados would agree that it would most probably comprise the following players: George Sisler, first base; Rogers Hornsby, second base; Honus Wagner, shortstop; Pie Traynor, third base; Babe Ruth, Ty Cobb, and Tris Speaker, outfield; Mickey Cochrane, catcher; Walter Johnson and Cy Young, righthanded pitchers; and Lefty Grove and Warren Spahn, lefthanded pitchers.

Ten of the 12 players performed for more than one team.

Hornsby played for five clubs; Young, four; Sisler, Ruth, and Spahn, three; and Wagner, Cochrane, Cobb, Speaker, and Grove, two.

Traynor played 17 years with the Pirates, and Johnson played 21 years with the Senators.

Dummy Hoy: Deaf and Dumb?

Dummy Hoy, a deaf and dumb outfielder for eight major league clubs around the turn of the century, was responsible for the umpires raising their hands on ball-and-strike calls.

When he was up at the plate, he could neither hear nor talk. So he continuously turned around to look at the umpire so that he could find out what the call was. The umpire would raise his right hand to signal a strike and his left hand to signal a ball.

Once the umpires started the practice, it caught on; they never stopped it!

The Born Baseball Loser

In life there are many born losers. But in baseball it's doubtful if there's ever been a bigger one than Fred Merkle.

Late in the 1908 season, Merkle pulled a boner when he failed to touch second base after Al Bridwell's "apparent" single had downed the Cubs and clinched the pennant for the Giants. But, in the midst of a pennant-winning celebration by the natives of Coogan's Bluff, Johnny Evers, the Cubs' second baseman, retrieved the ball, touched his base, and got the umpire to call Merkle out.

The game, which thereby ended in a tie, eventually had to be played off because the Giants lost their last five games and ended the season in a tie with Chicago. The Cubs won the playoff and earned the right to represent the National League in the 1908 World Series with the Tigers. Ever since that time, Merkle's mistake has gone down in the annals of baseball as "Merkle's Boner."

In 1912 the Giants might have won the World Series if Merkle had played heads-up baseball. In the bottom of the tenth inning of the seventh game, with the Giants winning 2-1, Speaker lifted an easy pop foul to first base with runners on first and second and one out. Merkle, who had the best chance at the ball, and catcher Chief Meyers let the ball drop between them; Speaker, presented with another chance, singled the tying run home and sent Josh Devore to third base. Larry Gardner's sacrifice fly, which should have been the third out, scored Devore with the winning run of the Series.

Babe Herman hit .393 in the 1930 season, but failed to win the batting championship because Bill Terry batted .401.

So Merkle was indirectly responsible for the Giants' losing both a pennant and a World Series.

A first baseman for all three New York teams, Merkle had the added misfortune of playing in five losing World Series with the Giants (3), the Dodgers (1), and the Cubs (1). He never played on a winning team in World Series play. In fact, he is the only player to have competed on five losing World Series teams without ever performing on a winning club.

He closed out his career with the Yankees in 1926. But he was dropped from the squad before the Bronx Bombers lost the World Series to the Cardinals. It might have been the biggest break he ever got!

The .330 Runners-Up

In addition to Joe Jackson, Riggs Stephenson and Eddie Collins have been the only two modern players who have averaged .330-or-better without winning a batting title.

Stephenson (.336) ended up fourth in the 1927 batting race. It was his best finish. Collins (.333) finished the runner-up to Ty Cobb three times: 1909, 1914, and 1915.

The Inseparable Teammates

Tris Speaker and Joe Wood were good. They were inseparable, too.

"The Grey Eagle" came up to the Red Sox in 1907; "Smoky Joe" joined him in 1908. They played in Boston until 1916. In 1912, when the Red Sox won both the pennant and the World Series, they both had their greatest year in the Hub: Speaker hit .383 and Wood won 37 games, including three in the seven-game series.

In 1916 Speaker was traded to Cleveland, where he became the playing manager in 1919; and Wood, who had hurt his arm, took a one-year leave of absence. But Wood once again joined his old buddy, Speaker, with the Indians in 1917. For six more years they were teammates. Wood switched from the mound to the outfield; so, day after day, he played side-by-side with the incomparable center fielder.

In 1920 they played together in another World Series. This time the club was managed by Speaker, though.

In 1921 and 1922 Wood hit .366 and .297, respectively. Then Wood hung up his spikes for good. Speaker stayed in the majors for another six years. But he had to look for another roommate. Wood, who played 14 years in the big leagues, had only one roomie in his entire career—Tris Speaker!

Speaker's Interruption

When does a major league hitter reach his peak?

Most major league players contend that the prime batting years for athletes on the diamond are between 28 and 32. But if the late Tris Speaker, considered one of the three greatest outfielders ever, were questioned on the subject, he would most probably say that a hitter reaches his peak between 32 and 37.

During that span "The Grey Eagle" batted for a .374 average. Over a 22-year playing career, the former playing manager for the Cleveland Indians hit *only* .344.

Five times in his career, Speaker hit .380-or-better. In 1925 at the age of 37, he batted .389. No one before or since has hit that high at that advanced baseball age. But he won only one batting title. That's because he had the misfortune of playing during the heyday of Ty Cobb, also one of the three greatest outfielders who ever lived. (The other one, of course, is Babe Ruth.)

But in 1916, when Speaker won the batting title with an average of .386, Cobb wished that the Tribe's nonpareil flyhawk were playing in another era. "The Georgia Peach" finished second in batting that year with a mark of .371. Speaker's batting title broke a string of nine consecutive hitting crowns for Cobb, who proceeded to run off three more batting championships from 1917-19.

Had Speaker not interrupted Cobb's string of titles, the Detroit firebrand would have won an unbelievable 13 straight batting championships!

Crawford and Cobb: A Duo who Hit Triples

There have been some great home run hitters who batted three-four in different line-ups: Babe Ruth and Lou Gehrig, Eddie Mathews and Hank Aaron, Mickey Mantle and Roger Maris, and Willie Mays and Willie McCovey, to name a few.

A good argument would be as to which of the pairs was the most awesome.

But when the topic turns to triples, there can be no argument as to which three-four hitters were the best: Ty Cobb and Sam Crawford. Between them the two Tigers' outfielders won ten triples championships. Crawford won six; Cobb, four.

Overall, Crawford hit 312 triples, the all-time high; Cobb, 297, the second all-time high. Between them they hit a total of 609 triples!

The National League's Babe Ruth

Only Ralph Kiner has won more home run titles in the National League than Gavvy Cravath, who played most of his 11-year career in the Phillies outfield.

Cravath, who batted .287 lifetime, won the home run title six times. That ties for the second best home run ratio to Kiner. Mel Ott won the title six times also. Kiner won seven home run titles in ten years.

In 1919, Cravath's next-to-last year, he won his sixth-and-last home run crown with 12 four-base blows. The unusual thing about Cravath's 1919 season was that he played only 83 games and appeared at the plate only 212 times.

Benny Kauff, the Giants' outfielder who finished second in the home run derby that year with ten, came to the plate 491 official times.

Cravath's 212 at-bats in 1919 were the least number of plate appearances by a player in the year that he won the home run crown!

The Clandestine Clan

Students of the game of baseball know that Joe Jackson, Buck Weaver, Ed Cicotte, and five other members of the White Sox were officially banned from professional diamonds after the 1920 season because of circumstantial evidence that linked them to a possible fix of the 1919 World Series.

But only true aficionados of the sport know that one year earlier Hal Chase and Heinie Zimmerman, two of the finest players of their day, were unofficially barred from the National Pastime for alleged betting on and against their own teams.

Chase, a .291 lifetime hitter, began his career with the Highlanders in 1905 and finished it 15 years later with the Giants in 1919. "Prince Hal" is still acknowledged as the best fielding first baseman who ever played the game.

But he had a penchant for games of chance, and it caused his undoing. Christy Mathewson, his manager with the Reds, released him after the 1918 season because of rumors that connected Chase with manipulating baseball games. John McGraw, always willing to believe the best about a person, picked him up for the 1919 season. But, by the end of the year, McGraw had suspicions of his own and dropped him from his team.

Chase, though he hit .284 in 1919, was not picked up by any other major league team.

Zimmerman, a .295 lifetime hitter, was one of the best second basemen during his 13-year career from 1907-19. In 1912 the Cubs' second sacker led the league in batting (.372), hits (207), and home runs (14).

In time he led the league in gossip about the honesty of his play, too. Finally, a Giants' pitcher told McGraw that Zimmerman had offered him money to "lose the game." McGraw suspended Zimmerman the following day. Somewhat later Zimmerman signed an affidavit that attested he had successfully bribed three Giants' teammates. But ultimately they were exonerated.

No formal charges were ever filed against Chase or Zimmerman, who ended their careers in the same year under a cloud. But it's relatively safe to say that they were "chased" from baseball!

Jackson: Shoeless and Luckless

Joe Jackson didn't have too much luck in baseball.

In 1911, as a rookie, he batted .408, the highest average ever turned in by a freshman major league player. But he finished second in the American League batting race. Ty Cobb won the crown with a mark of .420, his all-time high.

One year later, "Shoeless Joe" *slipped* to .395. Cobb *slipped*, too. But .410 was still good enough to distance Jackson's second-place finish.

In the 1919 World Series the White Sox outfielder led all the hitters in the Fall Classic with an average of .375. But one year later he was indicted, along with seven other Chicago players, for conspiracy to throw the series.

Baseball Commissioner Kenesaw Landis banned the eight "Black Sox" from baseball for the rest of their lives because of "conduct detrimental" to the national pastime, although all were acquitted by a civil court.

In 1920, his last in the big leagues, Jackson hit a remarkable .382. He finished third in the batting race, though. George Sisler led the loop with an average of .407, and Tris Speaker pounded the ball at a .388 clip.

Over a 13-year career Jackson hit .356. Only Ty Cobb (.367) and Rogers Hornsby (.358) did better. Cobb won 12 batting titles; Hornsby, seven. But Jackson never won a league batting crown.

In fact, of the eight players who have hit .400, he was the only one who never did so!

Over a 13-year career Joe Jackson hit .356. Only Ty Cobb and Rogers Hornsby have done better, but Jackson failed to win even one league batting crown.

A Sunny Start

"Sunny Jim" Bottomley had good reason to be cheerful about the first ten years of his 16 years in the big leagues: he hit better than .300 in every season except 1926, when he batted .299.

Consistency was Bottomley's trademark. Twice he hit safely six times in six times at bat. The only other player who has equalled this feat was Roger "Doc" Cramer. From 1924-29 he drove home better than 100 runs in six straight seasons. Twice during that time he led the league in doubles; once he paced the loop in triples; and once he headed the circuit in homers. From 1926-31 he played in four Wold Series with the Cardinals.

Overall, he batted .310 and hit 217 home runs.

But the most exceptional game he ever had occurred during the 1924 season: in that game he drove home 12 runs. No one, before or since, has equalled his feat!

Hornsby's Hitting Spree

Rogers Hornsby, who played second base for 23 years, was undoubtedly the greatest righthanded hitter of all time.

"The Rajah" won a total of seven league batting titles. Honus Wagner leads the senior circuit with eight crowns. Only Ty Cobb, a lefty, won more — 12. Hornsby won six consecutive league batting crowns. Only Cobb won more—9. The one-time playing manager of the Cardinals won two Triple Crowns. Only Ted Williams, a lefty, equalled the feat.

But Hornsby accomplished what no other player did. He set team batting highs for three different teams: the Cardinals, .424 in 1924; the Braves, .387 in 1928; and the Cubs, .380 in 1929. He also hit .403 over a five-year period (1921-25); his averages were .397, .401, .384, .424, and .403.

The highest that Cobb ever hit over a five-year stretch was .396.

The MVP Jinx

Most major league players covet the Most Valuable Player Award. But it turned out to be a jinx for the Senators' Roger Peckinpaugh, who won it in 1925.

A .294 hitter during the regular season, he was named the MVP before the World Series. In the Senators' World Series victory over the Giants the preceding fall, Peckinpaugh had hit a torrid .417. But in the Nats' loss to the Pirates in 1925, his average slipped to a mediocre .250. In that same series the Senators' shortstop committed eight errors — a record.

The following year Peckinpaugh's average dipped to .238. One year later, he was traded to the White Sox. By the end of the season, he had faded from the major league scene.

Since 1925 the MVP in each league has been named after — not before — the World Series!

Cobb's Batting Slump

Ty Cobb, who won a record 12 batting titles, including nine in succession, batted .363 over the last nine years of his career; yet he failed to win a batting crown.

In the last 20 years the only American League player who has batted better than .363 in a season is Rod Carew, who hit .364 in 1974 and .388 in 1977!

Baseball's Biggest Headache

Wally Pipp had the most costly headache in the history of baseball.

In 1925, his twelfth season in the majors, he was regarded as one of the best first basemen in all of baseball. Twice he had won the league's home run championship; three times he had batted better than .300. So he might have assumed that he deserved a rest from time to time. Midway through the 1925 season, he asked manager Miller Huggins if he might have the day off because of a nagging "headache." Huggins, granting his wish, inserted young Lou Gehrig into Pipp's spot in the lineup. No first baseman got Gehrig out of the lineup for 2,130 games. "The Iron Horse" didn't miss a game for 14 seasons. In 1926 Pipp moved on to Cincinnati and played the last three years of his career with the Reds.

During those three years the Yankees won three pennants and two world championships. Whenever Pipp thought of the World Series money that he had blown, he got a headache. A real one!

Simmons's Bucketful of Ribbies

Al Simmons, the hard-hitting left fielder for the Athletics, hit .384 in 1925 and .392 in 1927; and in both of those years he failed to win the batting title. That's because Harry Heilmann of the Tigers hit .393 and .398.

Later, in 1930-31, when Heilmann was in the twilight of his career, Simmons won back-to-back titles when he hit .381 and .390.

"Bucketfoot Al," who played 20 years in the majors, was one of the hardest-hitting right-handed batters in the big leagues. Lifetime, he batted .334 and belted 307 home runs.

In 1925, his second season in the majors, he collected 253 hits, the third highest total in history. During a five-year stretch, 1929-33, he amassed 200-or-more hits in each season to become the only player to collect that many hits in five consecutive seasons.

In his first 11 seasons in the major leagues (1924-34) he drove home 100-or-more runs in each season. No other player has done that, either!

The Sultan of Swat

It's amazing just how fantastic Babe Ruth's home run production was.

In "The Sultan of Swat's" first four years with the Yankees (1920-23), he hit 189 home runs, which was two more than all of the league leaders from 1901-19 had totalled.

In 1927 he clouted 60 homers, a record which stood over 34 years. During that record-setting year he hit more personal home runs than any team other than the Yankees hit collectively. The Yankees, with Ruth and Gehrig (49) leading the way, hit a league-leading total of 158. The Athletics ended up second with a team total of 56.

Ruth's slugging dominance is further illustrated when one realizes that Tony Lazzeri ended up third in the home run race that year with a total of 18 four-base blows.

"The Bambino" hit more than three times the number of home runs than did the number-three home run hitter in the league!

Batting Deflation

Inflation may be at an all-time high in America, but deflation is at an all-time low in baseball: never in the history of the game has the batter been getting more for his base hit than he is today.

Take Carl Yastrzemski, for example. In the 1960s he won three batting titles with averages of .321, .326, and .301, respectively.

Between 1928 and 1930 when Babe Herman of the Dodgers was in his prime, he couldn't win a batting crown with successive averages of .340, .381, and .393. In fact, although he batted .324 for 13 years, he never did win a batting title.

The batting champs from 1928-30 were Rogers Hornsby, Lefty O'Doul, and Bill Terry: they batted .387, .398, and .401, respectively!

The Boy Wonder

It's no wonder baseball followers called Mel Ott "The Boy Wonder."

At the age of 17, he played his first game in the major leagues. At the age of 20, he hit 42 home runs, the highest total of four-base blows ever hit by a player that age or younger.

Gene Tenace set a record when he clouted home runs in his first two official appearances in World Series play.

26

Six times he won the National League home run title. Ralph Kiner, who won seven league titles, has been the only senior circuit player who has won it more times than Ott. Kiner and Ott share another record: each tied for the league's home run lead three times. Over a 22-year major league playing career, Ott hit a total of 511 home runs, the most circuit clouts that have been hit by a left-handed National League player.

But the unusual aspect of Ott's home run record is that he did not win the title when he hit 42 base-clearing blows in 1929. Chuck Klein of the Phillies hit 43 homers to lead the league. Never again did Ott approach 42 home runs. His next highest total was 38. But he did win six home run crowns!

Batting Inflation

The live ball hit its peak in 1930.

Six of the National League teams had club batting averages of better than .300; three of the American League clubs had team batting averages of better than .300. The Junior Circuit had a league batting average of .288; the Senior Circuit had a league average of .303. The 16 major league teams had a combined average of .296.

In that same year the Phillies had a team batting average of .315, the third highest in history; and the Giants had a club batting average of .319, the all-time high!

Farewell Address

Many baseball players break into the big leagues with a bang. But by the time that they depart from the majors, their bats have become heavy and silent.

Bill Terry, the last National League player who hit .400 in a season (.401 in 1930), was an exception to that general rule. It took "Memphis Bill" four years to gain his stroke; but once he did, he never lost it. The highest hitting first baseman in the history of the game (.341), Terry finished off his 14-year major league career with ten consecutive .300 seasons!

Batting Champs on the Move

David Dale Alexander and Harry Walker were the only two players who have won the batting championship while members of two teams.

"Moose" Alexander, who came up to the big leagues with the Tigers in 1929, won the batting title in 1932 when he hit .363 for the Tigers and the Red Sox, to whom he was traded after he appeared in 23 games for Detroit.

Harry "The Hat" started his major league career in 1940 with the Cardinals and copped the hitting crown in 1947 when he compiled a .363 average for the Redbirds and the Phillies, to whom he was traded after he appeared in ten games for St. Louis.

There are other similarities between Alexander and Walker.

Alexander broke into the majors with a bang, hitting .343 and slugging 25 home runs in his rookie season. But his figures kept declining. In his sophomore year he batted .326 and belted 20 homers. One year later, he hit .325. But his home run total plummeted to three. Both figures came up in 1932. Besides winning the batting title, he raised his four-base output to eight. But in 1933, both figures dropped once again: he hit .281 and tagged just five home runs.

In 1934 he was out of baseball. His lifetime batting average was .331. Yet he played only five years in the big leagues.

In 1942, Walker's first full year, he hit a solid .314. The next two years his batting average slid to .294 and .237. (He did miss two seasons in between those years because of the service.) Then in his fourth full season, just like Alexander, he won the batting crown. Walker played four more seasons in the majors, never again with the success he realized in 1947, but his total appearances at the plate added up to only two regular full seasons.

Overall, Alexander had 2,450 official at-bats in the majors; Walker had 2,650. These two batting champions logged an average of just about four full seasons in the big time!

The Hitter who Pitchers Couldn't Strike Out

Henry Aaron, Babe Ruth, Willie Mays, and Jimmy Foxx were super hitters and sluggers. Yet they did not have great bat control. Each of them went down swinging at least 60 times per season.

Ted Williams, Stan Musial, and Joe DiMaggio were super hitters and sluggers, too. Yet they had great bat control. None of the three averaged more than 37 strikeouts per season.

Williams, who batted .344 with 521 home runs, struck out the most of the three. He fanned an average of 37 times a year. In 1939 his rookie year, he struck out 64 times, his most, and in 1941, the year he hit .406, he whiffed 27 times, his least.

Musial, who batted .331 with 475 home runs, averaged 32 whiffs a season. His top number was 46 in 1962, his next-to-last season, and his bottom figure was 18 in 1943, the year he won his first of six batting titles.

DiMaggio, who batted .325 with 361 home runs, struck out the least of the three—28 times a year. In 1936, his rookie season, he fanned 39 times, his most, and in 1941, the year he batted safely in 56 consecutive games, he breezed 13 times, his least.

When baseball people talk about bat control, they begin and end the conversation with the name of Joe Sewell, who batted .312 and hit 49 home runs during his career with the Indians and Yankees. Sewell's most strikeouts in one season were 20 in 1922. His low figure was three! He did that twice: in 1930 and 1932. Three times he struck out only four times in a year.

Over a 14-year career Sewell struck out only 114 times. That's an average of eight times a year!

Triple Crown Twins

In 1933, in the depths of the Depression, there was no slugging shortage in Philadelphia: Chuck Klein of the Phillies and Jimmy Foxx of the A's both won the Triple Crown.

Overall, there have been ten players who have won a total of

12 Triple Crowns: Ty Cobb, Rogers Hornsby, Klein, Foxx, Lou Gehrig, Joe Medwick, Ted Williams, Mickey Mantle, Frank Robinson, and Carl Yastrzemski. Hornsby and Williams are the only players who have won it twice.

But only once have two players won the Triple Crown in the same year; and in that year both of the players came from the same city — Philadelphia.

But it was not the only time that one city had captured the top three batting awards in one year. In 1922 Hornsby swept all three honors in the National League for the St. Louis Cardinals. In the same year, however, George Sisler of the St. Louis Browns won the American League batting title; and Ken Williams of the Browns won both the home run and RBI titles!

Rice: A Victim of the Numbers Game

Sam Rice was one of many great baseball players victimized by the numbers game.

The Senators' outfielder ended his 20-year career with a lifetime average of .322 and total of 2,987 hits, just 13 short of the magic 3,000 mark. Rice, who had hit .293 and collected 98 hits, elected to retire after the 1934 season. Records weren't too important in his day. But if he were playing today, he undoubtedly would have played for an extra year and ended up with 3,000 hits.

Those 13 hits cost him baseball immortality.

Ironically, Rice is remembered today more for a controversial defensive play he made in the 1925 World Series against the Pirates, than for his consistent bat. Rice made a backhand grab of Earl Smith's line drive in right center field. But his momentum carried him into the right field seats. There were many people who believed that Rice dropped the ball. The umpires ruled he didn't. The Senators won the game, 4-3, but lost the World Series, 4-3.

Forty years later, Rice wrote a letter describing the details of the play, and mailed it to Paul Kerr, President of the National
30

Baseball Hall of Fame and Museum. He directed Kerr to open the letter after his death and reveal the contents of it to the members of the press. When Rice died in 1974, his wishes were followed.

The essence of the letter was: "My feet hit the barrier . . . and I toppled over on my stomach into (sic) first row of bleachers . . . at no time did I lose possession of the ball."

Not only was he the fielding star of the 1925 World Series, but he led both teams with 12 hits!

The G-Men

The G-Men were one of the most dependable trios of the 1930s Hank Greenberg, Charley Gehringer, and Goose Goslin.

The person who depended on them the most was Mickey Cochrane, manager of the Tigers. In 1934 and 1935 they led his teams to back-to-back pennants. In 1934 the three sluggers hit for a collective average of .333; they drove home an average of 122 runs. In 1935 the three Bengals batted .317 and drove home 124 runs each. Careerwise, Gehringer hit .320; Goslin, .316; and Greenberg, .313.

The Tigers had some powerful hitters in the 1930s.

In 1937 four of them got 200 hits in one season: Greenberg, Gehringer, Pete Fox, and Gee Walker. That's the only time that four players on the same team have had 200 hits in the same season.

In 1934 the Tigers' infield of Greenberg, Gehringer, Billy Rogell, and Marv Owen set a record, too: they drove home a total of 462 runs. The only member of the infield who didn't reach the 100 mark was Owen. He delivered *only* 96.

But the three players who drew the most attention then—and later — were the G-men: Greenberg, Gehringer, and Goslin. Today they are all enshrined in the Hall of Fame.

The Pitchers' "Ache and Pain"

Luke Appling, who won two batting titles, is the only White Sox player who has copped two hitting championships: he won the crown in 1936 when he hit .388, and he repeated in 1943 when he batted .328.

Although he batted .300 in 16 of his 20 seasons, "Old Aches and Pains" never again came close to the .388 he posted in 1936. That year he hit two other personal highs, too: he accumulated 204 hits and he drove home 128 runs.

The RBI total is an incredible statistic. For Appling hit only six home runs in 1936. In fact, he hit only 45 round-trippers in his entire career. That's an average of 2.25 per season!

Double-X a Triple-X Winner

Ed Delahanty won a batting title in each league, Sam Crawford won a home run title in each league, and Frank Robinson won a Most Valuable Player Award in each league. But Jimmy Foxx copped each of those distinctions in the same league.

In 1899 Delahanty hit .410 for the Phillies. Traded to the American League, he led the Junior Circuit in 1902 when he hit .376 for the Senators. Crawford paced the Senior Circuit with 16 home runs in 1901. Seven years later, he paced the American League with the modest total of seven for the Tigers. Robinson copped the MVP Award in 1961 with the Reds, the year they won the pennant. He also won it with the Orioles in 1966, the year he won the Triple Crown and the year the Orioles swept the Dodgers in four games in the series.

Foxx performed all three. In 1933 he paced the American League in hitting with a .356 average for the Athletics. Traded off to the Red Sox, by Connie Mack, he won it again in 1938 with a mark of .349. Foxx was a three-time home run champ with the A's: 58 in 1932, 48 in 1933, and 36 in 1935. He was a one-time four-base champ with the Red Sox: 35 in 1939. He won three MVP awards, too. In 1932 and 1933 he was honored with the A's; in 1938 he was singled out with the Red Sox.

Jimmy Foxx was the only player who has won the batting championship, the home run title, and the MVP Award with two different teams!

32

A .300 Hitter

Ethan Allen, who played on six teams during his 13-year career, was one of the good hitters who wasn't appreciated.

He hit .300 for four of those teams: the Reds, the Giants, the Phillies, and the Browns.

Fittingly, he ended his career with a .300 lifetime average!

The Catch to Catching

Only two catchers have ever won a batting crown: Eugene Hargrave and Ernie Lombardi, the only backstop who has won it *twice*, and with two different teams.

Hargrave, who batted .310 during a 12-year career with the Cubs, Reds, and Yankees, hit .353 in 1926 to win the batting crown while he played for Cincinnati.

Lombardi, who batted .306 during a 17-year career with the Dodgers, Reds, Braves, and Giants, hit .342 for Cincinnati in 1938, and he hit .330 for the Braves in 1942.

No catcher in the American League has ever won a batting title!

Greenberg: An Homeric Deception

When you look at Hank Greenberg's home run total of 331, you see he is sandwiched between Joe Adcock (336) and Roy Sievers (318). But don't ever deceive yourself into thinking that Adcock and Sievers were in the same home run class as Greenberg!

Big Hank hit .313 for 13 seasons. During that span he won four home run titles. In 1938 he hit 58 four-base blows. One year he hit 63 doubles, four less than the all-time high held by Earl Webb. Another year he drove home 183 runs, one less than the American League high held by Lou Gehrig.

The amazing thing about Greenberg's home run total is that he missed five and one-half years of his career because of injury and military service. In 1936 he broke his wrist and missed practically the whole season. During the Second World War he missed four and one half seasons.

In 1935 he hit 36 home runs; in 1937 he hit 40. So it is relatively safe to assume that, if Greenberg had been healthy in 1936, he would have hit close to 38 four-base blows. In 1940, the year before he left for the service, he clouted 41 round-trippers; in 1946, the first full season he had after he returned from the service, he smacked 44 circuit clouts. It seems safe to assume, if we once again split the difference, that Greenberg would have averaged 42.5 home runs per year for the five years he missed during the War. Add those figures to his total of 331 homers, and you come out with a figure of 581.

Greenberg was a tremendous clutch player, too. He demonstrated that forcefully on the last day of the 1945 season. Discharged from the service midway through the season, the .311-hitting Greenberg was just beginning to gain his stride. With the Tigers losing to the Browns, 2-1, in the top of the ninth, Greenberg homered with the bases loaded to clinch the championship for the Tigers.

Eliminate the 1936 season when he was injured, and you find that Greenberg led the League in home runs in three of the five years before he entered the service. Include 1946, the first year of his return, and you learn that he paced the Junior Circuit in home runs in four of his last six full seasons.

How many home run titles would Greenberg have won had he played those extra five and one half years? Who knows? It's almost as difficult as speculating why the Tigers let him go to the Pirates in 1947 after he led the American League in home runs, with 44, and RBI, with 127 in 1946. But it turned out that the Tigers' front office knew what it was doing. "Hammerin' Hank" hit only 25 home runs in his final year and batted just .249, the lowest of his career.

With the Pirates, however, he taught a rookie the ideal home run swing. That freshman player was Ralph Kiner, who led the National League in home runs the first seven years of his major league career. No one else, not even Babe Ruth, has led a league in home runs for seven consecutive years.

Wes Ferrell was a great pitcher and a great slugger. He holds the all-time home-run lead for pitchers, with 38 four-base blows.

Overall, Kiner hit 369 home runs in a ten-year career for a 37 home runs per-season average. But don't confuse Kiner with Greenberg. One was the teacher, the other the student!

Four-Decade Players

Three ballplayers who came up to the major leagues in 1939 extended their careers over four decades: Ted Williams, Mickey Vernon, and Early Wynn.

Williams, who hit .344 lifetime, debuted and departed from the major leagues in similar fashion: in 1939 he batted .327 and banged 31 home runs; in 1960 he hit .316 and stroked 29 home runs. Overall, he batted .344 and slugged 521 four-base blows.

Vernon, a talented first baseman, was the most inconsistent of the three. Twice he won the batting championship. In 1946 he hit .353 and in 1953 he batted .337. Yet he wound up his 20-year career with a lifetime batting average of .286 — good but not befitting a batter who had won two hitting championships.

Wynn had the longest active career of the three. In between a humble start (0-2) and a modest finish (1-2), "Gus" enjoyed a great career. Five times he won 20 games in a season. In 1963, his last season, he won only one game for the Indians. But it just happened to be his 300th. And he got it in relief.

Williams went out in dramatic fashion, too. In his last at-bat in the major leagues, he hit a home run off Jack Fisher. To Williams there was little difference between the pitchers of the 1930s, whom he faced as a rookie, and the moundsmen of the 1960s, whom he eyed at the ripe old age of 42.

They all had to put the ball over the plate. And no one knew the strike zone any better than Ted Williams!

The Bronx Bombers

There have been many great outfields in baseball. But, from the standpoint of slugging consistency in one year, it would be hard to find a better one than the Yankees' outfield of Tommy Henrich, Joe DiMaggio, and Charlie Keller in 1941.

Between them they averaged .311, 31 home runs, and 111 runs batted in.

Each one of them hit 30-or-more home runs: Keller, 33; Henrich, 31; and DiMaggio, 30!

DiMaggio: The "Streak" Hitter

When baseball people talk about a "streak" hitter, they mean an inconsistent one. When baseball people say that Joe DiMaggio was a "streak" hitter, though, they mean that, day in and day out, he was unbelievably *consistent*.

In 1941, of course, DiMaggio hit safely in 56 consecutive games to set a major league record. It would have gone much further had not Kenny Keltner, the third baseman for the Indians, made two remarkable plays to take base hits away from him. DiMaggio started another streak the next day: he hit safely in 17 consecutive games. If Keltner had not made those sensational plays, DiMaggio would have extended his batting streak to 74 games—three shy of one-half a season.

What many people don't know is that DiMaggio owns the longest batting streak in the Pacific Coast League, too. In 1935, with the San Francisco Seals, he hit safely in 61 consecutive games!

The Last of the .400 Hitters

Ted Williams was the last major leaguer who hit .400 in a season. He was also the last player—besides Rod Carew who batted .388 in 1977—who came closest to hitting .400.

In 1941 he hit .406. It was the first time a player had hit .400 since Bill Terry of the Giants batted .401 in 1930. In 1957, at the age of 37, he hit .388.

What many baseball fans don't know, is that Williams hit .400 on two other occasions, too. In 1952, before he left for the Korean War, he batted .400 in ten official trips to the plate. In 1953, after his return from the Korean War, he hit .407 in 91 official trips to the plate.

In both of those fragmented seasons he got 41 hits in 101 official at-bats for a .406 average, the same figure he had hit in 1941 to become the last player to *officially* bat .400 in a season!

For Whom the Bell Tolls

There were many ballplayers whose careers were affected by the Second World War. Some of them failed to register 3,000 hits because of the interruption in their careers. Others didn't reach the 300-win column because of the gap in their playing days. But Cecil Travis didn't make an all-time team because of the intermission in his career.

Travis was primarily a shortstop, although he played third base early in his career because Joe Cronin, the league's all-time shortstop, played the pivot position for the Senators. Cronin also happened to be the team's manager.

But after the 1934 season, owner Clark Griffith, who just happened to be Cronin's father-in-law, sold Cronin to the Red Sox for $250,000. Griffith then moved Travis to shortstop. In his first eight full seasons in the majors, Travis hit .300 seven times and compiled a .326 lifetime average. In 1941 he batted .359, his all-time high. But, at the height of his career, he was called into the service.

When he was discharged from the service, he never regained his top playing form. In 15 games in 1945, he batted a sub-par .241. And the sub-par performances continued. The following year, he batted .252; and in 1947, his last year, he dipped to .214. His post-war batting average was .233, nearly 100 points below his pre-war batting average.

If he had been able to continue to play in 1942, he probably would have continued to hit .300 for at least several more years; and he most probably would be considered the American League's all-time shortstop today. Because Travis, although he probably lost his best four years to the service, recorded a lifetime average of .314, which is 12 points higher than Cronin's career average. It is also higher than any other American League   shortstop's lifetime batting average!

38

Pinch-Hit Power

When baseball followers think in terms of long-ball-hitting pinch-hitters, they automatically visualize images of Jerry Lynch and Bob Cerv. But when they think of pinch-hitters who were outstanding long-ball hitters for one single season, they zero in on Johnny Frederick of the Dodgers and Joe Cronin of the Red Sox.

Frederick, who established a .308 lifetime average in six seasons with Brooklyn, in 1932 had an extraordinary pinch-hitting year. He connected safely nine times in 29 trips to the plate. What is amazing, however, is that six of those hits were home runs — a major league record that has endured for 45 years. Overall, his pinch-hitting lifetime average was .306, two points shy of his overall career average.

Cronin was consistent, too. Lifetime, he batted .302. Part-time, he hit .288. In his first 16 years in the big leagues, he pinch-hit only 13 times. In his last three full seasons in the majors, he pinch-hit 91 times. Twenty-eight times in those 91 tries, he hit safely. That adds up to .308.

But in 1943 he outdid himself. He hit safely 18 times in 42 at-bats for a .429 average. What is amazing about his feat, however, is that five of those hits were home runs — an American League record that has lasted for 34 years.

In 1943 Cronin set another record: he hit home runs in a pinch-hitting role in both ends of a doubleheader. No one, before or since, has duplicated his feat!

The Best Candidate with the Least Votes

The Yankees have had three catchers who have been the recipients of the Most Valuable Player Award: Yogi Berra, Elston Howard, and Thurman Munson.

Berra was one of six players who have won the MVP Award three times. The other players who equalled Berra's feat were Jimmy Foxx, Joe DiMaggio, Stan Musial, Roy Campanella, and Mickey Mantle. The Yankees' catcher won the award in 1951, 1954, and 1955.

Howard won the honor in 1963 and Munson copped it in 1976.

Lifetime, the Yankees' catchers posted the following batting averages: Berra, .285; Howard, .274; and Munson, .291.

Ironically, the Yankees' backstop who recorded the highest lifetime batting average never won the MVP Award — Bill Dickey. In a 17-year career he batted .313!

Home-Run Stalemates

Seventeen times a league home run race has ended in a tie. The American League has had five stalemates while the National League has had 12 standoffs.

In the American League Babe Ruth and Harmon Killebrew tied for the home run title the most times — twice. In 1918 Ruth tied Tilly Walker of the A's and in 1931 teammate Lou Gehrig. In 1959 Killebrew equalled Rocky Colavito's total with the Indians and in 1967 Carl Yastrzemski's figure with the Red Sox.

Dave Robertson of the Giants was the first player to end up back-to-back seasons in home run ties: in 1916 he shared the honors with Cy Williams of the Cubs, and in 1917 he split the laurels with Gavvy Cravath of the Phillies.

Ralph Kiner of the Pirates and Johnny Mize of the Giants also finished back-to-back seasons in home run ties. But they tied each other. In 1947 Kiner and Mize each hit 51 home runs; in 1948 both of them hit 40.

Kiner also tied Hank Sauer of the Cubs for the home run lead in 1952, to become the second player to tie the four-base high three times. The first person who ended up in three ties for the league lead was Mel Ott, who deadlocked Chuck Klein of the Phillies in 1932, Rip Collins of the Cardinals in 1934, and Joe Medwick of the Cardinals in 1937.

If in 1946 Johnny Mize had hit one more home run, he and Kiner would have ended three consecutive seasons in a dead heat for the home run derby. Kiner hit 23 homers. Mize, who broke his wrist midway through the season, hit 22.

Over a three-year span only one home run separated the super sluggers!

Less than a Peach of an Outfielder

Ty Cobb may have been the best hitting center fielder who has ever lived. But he wasn't the best fielding center fielder who has ever lived.

"The Georgia Peach," whose lifetime fielding average was .961, averaged 12 errors per season for 23 years. In his worst season in the field, he committed 22 errors; in his best, he committed six.

By way of contrast, Joe DiMaggio posted a fielding average of .978 over a 13-year career. He committed an average of eight errors per season. In his worst season he made 17 errors; in his best season he made *one* .

"The Yankee Clipper's" fielding average in 1947, his best season, was .997!

Williams: The Number-Two Man

When Ted Williams did things, he liked to do them in twos.

"The Splendid Splinter" won six batting titles. Three times he won them back-to-back. He copped the crown in 1941-42, 1947-48, and 1957-58. Two of his four home run titles — 1941-42 —also came back-to-back. That made him the only player to win consecutive batting and home run laurels in the same years.

In 1947 he turned in another impressive "two." That was the year he won the Triple Crown for the second time. Only one other player has ever equalled that feat—Rogers Hornsby!

The Black Market

The National League jumped into the black market long before most American League clubs realized it was a profitable business. By the time the Junior Circuit woke up, the Senior Circuit had replaced it as the dominant league.

In 1947 both leagues initiated a combined Rookie of the Year Award. Jackie Robinson of the Dodgers was the initial winner. The following year, Al Dark of the Braves got the honor. In 1949 both leagues decided to give separate awards.

41

The first five awards in the National League (1949-53) went to black players: Don Newcombe, Sam Jethroe, Willie Mays, Joe Black, and Jim Gilliam. In six of the first seven years, black rookies were considered superior to their white counterparts by the National League.

The first black player who won the Rookie of the Year Award in the American League was Tony Oliva of Minnesota. That was in 1964!

Mapes: Making His Mark

Cliff Mapes (1948-52) was just a run-of-the-mill ballplayer (he batted .242 with 38 home runs); but he had the propensity to flirt, numerically speaking, with greatness.

When he came up to the Yankees in 1948, he was assigned Number 3. That was the number which the great Babe Ruth had worn for the Yankees. In 1948 on Babe Ruth Day, Number 3 was retired by the Yankees. So Mapes was assigned Number 7.

Midway through the 1951 season, Mapes was shipped to the Browns; and Mickey Mantle, a promising-looking rookie at the time, was given Number 7. Seventeen years later, the Yankees held a Mickey Mantle Day; naturally, on that day, Number 7 was retired.

That made Mapes the second baseball man in the history of the game who wore two numbers that were retired by the club for which he performed. Casey Stengel was the first — and the only other — baseballite who had two numbers retired. But Stengel, as always, was different. He had the same number retired twice; the Yankees retired Number 37 and the Mets retired Number 37.

Mapes was involved in another baseball rarity which affected another Bronx Bomber who ended up in the Hall of Fame — Joe DiMaggio.

On the last day of the 1949 season, with the Yankees and the Red Sox tied for first place, New York and Boston played for the pennant at Yankee Stadium. Going into the top of the ninth, the

Hank Aaron's 715th home run, Atlanta Stadium, April 8, 1974.

Yankees were leading, 5-1. But Vic Raschi, the Yankees' 20-game winner, tired; and the Red Sox reached him for two runs on a hit that cleared DiMaggio's head in center field — a rarity. DiMaggio normally would have had the ball; but he had just had viral pneumonia, and had come out in an attempt to inspire the Yankees to victory in their last two games with the Red Sox. He played courageously and well—three clutch hits in the two games — but he was still weak from his two-week illness.

So, with the pennant hanging in the balance, DiMaggio voluntarily removed himself from the game so that the Yankees could have a healthy center fielder. Casey Stengel replaced DiMaggio with Mapes, who caught a fly ball en route to the Yankees' 5-3 pennant-clincher. That pennant turned out to be the forerunner of five world championships at Yankee Stadium.

Lost in the shuffle of history is the fact that DiMaggio's removal from the game was an historical first: it was the first time in 11 major league seasons that he had been taken out of a game for a defensive replacement!

The Williams   Pass

Ted Williams, the last .400 hitter and a six-time batting titlist, never compiled 200 hits in one season!

The closest he ever came to 200 hits was in 1949, when he got 194 safeties, and 1940, when he reached 193.

There was a very good reason why "the Thumper" never reached that figure: opposing pitchers walked him a total of 2,018 times in 19 years. That divides out to 106 walks per season!

Fathers and Sons

Dixie Walker, Sr. had two sons who played major league baseball better than he; George Sisler had two sons who played major league baseball to a lesser degree than he did.

Dixie Walker, Sr. won 24 games and dropped 30 contests for the Senators from 1909-12. His sons, Dixie, Jr. and Harry, played the outfield with better success. Both of them won batting titles in the National League. They have been the only brothers to do so. Dixie hit .300 ten times; Harry, three.

George Sisler hit .340 during a 15-year career. Twice during his career he batted .400 and once he collected 257 hits, a major league record. He had two sons, Dick and Dave, who followed in his footsteps. Dick, who hit .276 lifetime with 55 home runs, played first base, as did his father. Dave, who had a career mark of 38-44, pitched, as did his father, when he first came up to the majors.

One of Dick's home runs, the three-run blast to left field in the tenth inning of the last game of the 1950 season, gave the Phillies the pennant, giving him the opportunity to play in a World Series.

His father, a Hall of Famer, never got that chance!

Rosen, the Third-Base Ribbie Man

The third baseman Al Rosen has been shortchanged by history.

"Flip" played only seven full seasons in the majors for the Indians, but those years were run-productive ones. For five consecutive years (1950-54) he drove home more than 100 runs each season. Lifetime, he averaged 102 RBI per season.

No other third baseman in baseball history has equalled his record!

Twelve Hits in a Row

Both Mike Higgins and Walt Dropo, each of whom played for the Tigers and the Red Sox, share   a more distinctive common bond: each got 12 consecutive hits, a major league record.

Higgins, who batted .292 lifetime, set the record with the Red Sox in 1938; and Dropo, who hit .270 lifetime, tied it with the Tigers in 1952.

The Brooklyn Brat

Eddie Stanky, it was said, couldn't run, throw, or hit: all he could do was beat you.

"The Brat" proved he was a winner between 1947-51. In 1947 he hit only .252. But he teamed up with Pee Wee Reese to give the Dodgers the defense they needed in the middle of the infield. And the Dodgers won the pennant!

In 1948 the Braves were looking for a veteran second baseman to team up with their promising rookie shortstop, Alvin Dark; so they made a deal for Stanky.

"Muggsy" didn't like leaving Brooklyn. But he didn't let it affect his play. He hit .320. Dark, who matured as a result of playing beside the shrewd Stanky, hit .322. And the Braves won the pennant!

In 1949 Leo Durocher of the Giants began to trade in his slugging for savvy. He got rid of Johnny Mize and Walker Cooper. Then, in 1950, he traded Sid Gordon, Willard Marshall, and Buddy Kerr to the Braves for the strength he sought up the middle: Stanky and Dark.

One year later, the trade paid off. Dark hit .303, Stanky .247. But the two excelled on defense and both hit 14 home runs. That was approximately half of Stanky's 11-year career total of 29. And the Giants won the pennant!

The following year, Stanky moved to St. Louis where he became a player-manager.

It may have been true that Stanky couldn't run, throw, or hit. But it was also true he could do the one thing they said he could do—beat you!

Thomson: One Step before Mays and Aaron

If a player has to be replaced in the lineup, he might as well be replaced by the best.

Bobby Thomson of the Giants was one of the best center fielders in the game during his tenure in New York from 1947 to 1953. He hit 179 home runs during that period. One of them—

"The Shot Heard Around The World" — decided the 1951 pennant. It decided the playoffs in the Giants' favor and sent the Dodgers down to bitter defeat in one of the most dramatic games of all time.

But "The Flying Scot," who hit 264 lifetime home runs, eventually had to move aside for two of the greatest home run hitters in baseball history: Willie Mays and Hank Aaron.

In 1951, when Mays came up to the Giants from Minneapolis, "The Seh Heh Kid" moved into the center field spot in the lineup while Thomson was switched to third base. Thomson never got his old spot back.

When he was traded to Milwaukee in 1954, the Braves inserted him in left field. But, midway through the season, he broke his ankle, and was replaced in the lineup by a promising rookie, Hank Aaron.

Thomson, in his time, was replaced by two players who went on to hit 1,415 career home runs.

But, when he returned to the lineup in 1955, he got his old position back. He played left field and Aaron switched to right field. So he might look at his association with Aaron in another light: he was the only player who ever replaced the home run king in the lineup!

Adcock's Afternoon

Joe Adcock, who hit .277 and 336 home runs during a 17-year stretch, hit some big ones during his career.

In 1954 he became one of a select number of batters to hit four home runs in one game. Evidently the Dodgers' pitching and the friendly fences of Ebbetts Field were to his liking.

In 1957 he drove home the only run of the fifth game of the World Series to give Lew Burdette a 1-0 victory over Whitey Ford.

And in 1959 he doubled home a run in the 13th inning to break up Harvey Haddix's no-hitter (he had a perfect game for 12 innings) and gave the Braves a 1-0 victory over the Pirates.

*Nap Lajoie was so esteemed by Cleveland fans that from 1905 to 1909
the club was nicknamed "Naps."*

But the biggest day in his career had to be that afternoon in Brooklyn when he hit four home runs and a double. It added up to 18 total bases—a major league record!

The Intentional Pass

Ted Williams was deprived of a batting title because opposing pitchers feared to face him.

That's right. In 1954, American League pitchers walked him 136 times, causing "The Splendid Splinter" to end up the season with 386 official times at bat, 14 less than the required 400. So Bobby Avila of the Indians won the batting title with an average of .341. Williams hit .345 but didn't qualify for the championship.

Today, in order to qualify for the batting title, a hitter has to have 502 plate appearances. If that rule had been in effect in 1954, Williams would have had 522 plate appearances, and would have been named the American League's batting champion!

The Rookie and the Pro

Al Kaline, who won a batting title at the age of 20, was the youngest player ever to have won it. Ted Williams, who won a batting crown at the age of 38, was the oldest player ever to have won it.

But Kaline, who was just starting out when he won the league title in 1955, never won another. Williams, who was coming to the end of the trail in 1958, had already won five!

The Heart of the Bums' Order

Rarely in the history of baseball has a team had such power in the middle of its lineup as had the Dodgers of the 1950s when they had Duke Snider, Gil Hodges, and Roy Campanella bat back-to-back.

From 1950-57, a period during which the Dodgers won four pennants and one world title, Snider, Hodges, and Campanella hit a total of 735 home runs—an average of 31 homers per man. Snider averaged 36; Hodges, 30; and Campanella, 25. From 1953-57 Snider hit 40-or-more home runs in each season.

During the same period they drove home a total of 2,471 runs, an average of 103 per man. Snider averaged 111; Hodges, 107; Campanella, 91. From 1950-55 Hodges drove home better than 100 runs in every season.

Yet, in their entire careers, they won only one home run title. In 1956 Snider led the league with 43.

Campy and Yogi: The Two Quarterbacks

Of the six players who have won the most valuable player award three times, Roy Campanella's record is the most amazing.

"Campy" won his three MVP honors during a ten-year career. All of the other three-time winners played at least 13 years in the majors.

In the early 1950s Campanella and Yogi Berra were the most singularly influential factors behind the repeated success of the Dodgers and Yankees. Over a five-year period (1951-55), they won a combined total of six MVP awards.

Berra won his awards in 1951, 1954, and 1955; Campanella in 1951, 1953, and 1955. They were the only catchers to win the MVP award in the same year. And they did it twice!

Bauer: A Winner from Start to Finish

A quick glance at Hank Bauer's baseball record might mislead one into thinking "Hammering Hank" was just an ordinary player. Not so. Hank Bauer, one of the greatest money players of all time, was a winner.

One could be deceived by his surface record, though. Overall, he batted .277 and hit 164 home runs during a 14-year career. In World Series play he hit .245 and batted seven home runs.

But, in Bauer's case, the record doesn't tell the whole story.

The first five full seasons that Bauer played in the majors, he spent on world championship teams. No other player has ever broken into the big time in such scintillating style. Overall, he played on nine pennant winners and seven world championships. In addition, in 1966 he managed the Orioles to a four-game sweep over the favored Dodgers.

Bauer could beat the opposition in many ways. He demonstrated them all in World Series play. Although he got off to a slow start with the bat in inter-league play, he came on strong in the stretch. In his first 80 trips to the plate, he recorded only 13 hits and just a .163 average. Up until his 112th appearance at the plate, he had only two extra base hits: both triples.

But the Yankees of Bauer's early years (1949-53) could afford to carry his anemic bat. They knew that, in time, it would get healthy. In the meantime, he was doing other things on the diamond that were helping them win.

In the sixth game of the 1951 World Series, he tripled three runs home to provide the margin of victory in the championship-clinching contest. Then, in the ninth inning, he thwarted a Giants' bid to tie the game when he made a sensational sliding catch on Sal Yvars' line drive.

One year later, he scored the winning run of the series when Billy Martin tallied him from second with a single to center field.

Suddenly, in 1955, he found his stroke: he hit the ball at a .429 clip. In his last four World Series he hit a consistent .306. From the first game of the 1956 until the third game of the 1958 World Series, he hit the ball safely in 17 consecutive games — a World Series record! In his last 78 times at-bat, during those three series, he clubbed seven home runs, an average of one every 11 times he came to the plate. He hit four home runs in the 1958 World Series (his last as a player) to tie a former record that was shared by Lou Gehrig, Babe Ruth, Duke Snider (twice), and Gene Tenace. (Reggie Jackson broke the record when he homered five times in the 1977 World Series.)

Some of those hits in the 17-game streak were clutch hits. In the sixth game of the 1957 World Series, he homered in the seventh inning to give the Yankees a 3-2 win over the Braves. In game three of the 1958 World Series, with the Braves up two games to none, Bauer drove in all four of the Yankees' runs in a 4-0 victory; he singled home two runs and he homered the other two home. During that series (which the Yankees won in seven games) Bauer homered in each of the first three games.

Eight years later, Bauer was back in a World Series, this time with the Orioles. But he could no longer win a game with a bat. So he relied on his formidable pitching staff, which literally took the bats out of the Dodgers' hands. The Birds' pitchers allowed only 17 hits, an average of four per game, and two runs, an average of one-half run per contest. In addition, they didn't permit a run over the last 33 innings of the series.

The Dodgers' team batting average of .142 during the 1966 World Series resembled Bauer's averages in his first five World Series. But there was one important difference: Bauer ended up with the lion's share of the series money; the Dodgers took the loser's end.

Hank Bauer bowed out of baseball, World-Series style, the way he broke in — a winner!

Mr. Cub

There were many reasons why the Chicago fans called Ernie Banks "Mr. Cub."

First, he hit 512 home runs. No other Bruin has hit that many four-base blows. In fact, no other combination shortstop-first baseman in the major leagues has hit that many. In 1958 he hit 47 home runs (the most ever hit by a shortstop) to lead the major leagues. Five times, he hit more than 40 home runs in a season. Forty is the second highest number of homers hit by a major league shortstop. Rico Petrocelli of the Red Sox hit them in 1969. Five times, Banks topped that.

In 1958 and 1959 Banks became one of nine National Leaguers to have won back-to-back RBI titles. He was the only member of the Cubs to have performed that feat. In fact, the only other shortstop in the history of baseball who has equalled that feat

Cy Young was probably the best pitcher ever and certainly the most durable one. He had a 22-year pitching career.

53

was Honus Wagner of the Pirates. Wagner did it twice (1901-02 and 1908-09).

"Mr. Cub" performed another unique feat. In 1969 at the age of 38, he drove home 106 runs. No other major leaguer has ever driven in that many runs at that age.

There was another reason why the Chicago fans called him "Mr. Cub." Every game he played for the Cubs, he considered a privilege. He never took the field without thinking that the Cubs would win the game.

Unfortunately, they didn't win enough: he was one of the very few players of his stature who never got the chance to play in a World Series!

The Clue to Big Klu's World Series

Ted Kluzewski, like Johnny Mize, moved from the National League to the American League when he was past his prime to become a World Series hero.

A .298 lifetime batter, "Klu" hit his peak between 1953 and 1956. During that period he hit 40-or-more home runs three times, he knocked in better than 100 runs every season, and he batted better than .300 every season. He averaged 43 home runs, 116 RBI, and .315.

After a back injury in 1957 his productivity fell off. Late in 1959, the White Sox picked him up; and the deal paid off immediately. "Klu" hit .293 down the stretch as the White Sox won their first pennant since 1920.

In the 1959 World Series against the Dodgers Kluzewski rose to the occasion. He hit .391 — three home runs and ten RBI, the most that any batter has driven home in a six-game series.

During the regular season he hit only four home runs, and he drove home just 27 RBI!

Cash: Off His Norm

Once in a while a player will get into a hot streak and play over his head.

In 1961 this happened to Norm Cash, the first baseman for the Tigers. That season Cash hit a sizzling .361 to win the American League batting title. He distanced the second-place finisher, teammate Al Kaline, by 37 points.

The remarkable thing about Cash's performance is that never before, or after, did he hit .300!

X-X and M-M

Two hitters with 50-or-more home runs in one season have failed to win the home run title the same year: Jimmy Foxx and Mickey Mantle!

Foxx, playing with the Red Sox, smashed 50 four-base blows in 1938. But Hank Greenberg of the Tigers distanced him in the home run derby with 58.

Mantle smacked 54 round trippers in 1961, the most that any hitter has ever clouted without winning the home run title. But fellow teammate Roger Maris lofted 61 home runs, the most times any player has ever circled the bases on a free ride.

Together in 1961, Mantle and Maris hit a total of 115 home runs — the most two players on the same team have ever hit in one season!

Maris and Wilson: Number One and Number Negative

Ten players in the history of baseball have hit 50-or-more home runs in a season. But Hank Aaron the number one, and Harmon Killebrew, the number five hitter on the all-time home run list, are not two of the ten!

Aaron's career high for one season was 47; Killebrew's 49. Eight times Aaron ended a season with a home run total in the 40s. That's the National League high. Eight times Killebrew wound up with a four-base total in the 40s. That's the American league high.

A comparison of Aaron's and Killebrew's overall home run totals and Roger Maris's and Hack Wilson's, the major league leaders for one season, is revealing.

Aaron finished his career with a major league total of 755 home runs; Killebrew with 573.

Roger Maris, who hit a major league high total of 61 in 1961, concluded a 12-year career with 275 home runs, less than half the total of either Aaron or Killebrew. Hack Wilson, who hit a National League high total of 56 in 1930, closed out his 12-year career with 244 home runs.

Overall, there have been 39 players who have hit 300-or-more lifetime home runs. Maris and Wilson were not two of them!

A Tale of Two Cities

Five players have hit 50-or-more home runs in a season more than once: Babe Ruth, Jimmy Foxx, Ralph Kiner, Mickey Mantle, and Willie Mays. But only two of them—Foxx and Mays—have hit 50-or-more home runs in more than one city.

Foxx hit 58 home runs for the Philadelphia A's in 1932 and 50 home runs for the Boston Red Sox in 1938. Mays hit 51 circuit clouts for the New York Giants in 1955 and 52 circuit clouts for the San Francisco Giants in 1965!

Tony "C"

By the time Tony Conigliaro of the red Sox was 22, he had already hit 104 home runs — more home runs than any other 22-year-old player had ever hit.

He did that despite a broken arm in 1964, his rookie year, and a ball in the eye in 1967. His first four-year home run totals were 24, 32, 28, and 20.

After a one-year layoff in 1968, he made a temporary come-back. For a while it seemed as though he had recovered from the eye injury. In 1969 he belted 20 home runs and in 1970, 36. But then his eye gave him trouble and he faded from the major leagues long before his time.

At the age of 22, Hank Aaron, Babe Ruth, and Willie Mays, the three greatest home run hitters in the history of the game, had hit the following number of circuit clouts: Aaron, 66; Ruth, 9; and Mays, 65!

Forty-Two Years of Hall of Fame Play

For 42 consecutive years center field in Yankee Stadium was patrolled by Hall of Fame players: Earle Combs (1924-35), Joe DiMaggio (1936-51), and Mickey Mantle (1952-66)!

DiMaggio, of course, missed the 1943-45 seasons while he was in the service; but he would have been in the starting line-up had not the War interrupted his career.

The three outfielders had many dissimilarities and many likenesses. Combs was a great on-base man, DiMaggio an unbelievable run producer, and Mantle a super slugger.

Combs, an ideal lead-off hitter, collected 200 hits in a season three times, including a club-high 231 in 1927. Lifetime, he batted .325.

Extraordinary as it may seem, DiMaggio turned in a career average of .325, too. So two outfielders who played the same position back-to-back for a total of 25 years finished their careers with the same lifetime average — .325.

But DiMaggio, who twice collected 200 hits in a season, was a great RBI man, too. He drove home 1537 runs in 13 seasons. That's an average of 118 RBI per season. It's also 28 more runs than Mantle drove home in 18 years. Mantle's season average was only 84. DiMaggio topped 100 RBI per season in each of his first seven years in the majors. Overall, he drove home 100 runs nine times. Mantle bettered 100 RBI in a season only four times.

Mantle was the superior home run hitter, though. He hit a total of 536 home runs. That averages out to 30 four-base blows per season. DiMaggio hit a total of 361 home runs, an average of 28 circuit clouts per year. Combs hit only 58 homers; an average of five per season.

But they do have some unusual features in common: they all played center field for the Yankees, they all played in succession, and they all ended up in Cooperstown. No other three players who are enshrined at the Hall of Fame fielded the same position, for the same team, over such a period of time!

Brothers who Could Bat

The Meusels, the Waners, the DiMaggios, and the Alous have been just about the four best hitting families in the major leagues.

Emil "Irish" and Bob Meusel each played the outfield for 11 seasons. In three of those years (1921-23) they played opposite to each other in the World Series. "Irish" played for the Giants and Bob for the Yankees. The Giants won the Autumn Classic in both 1921 and 1922; the Yankees in 1923.

They competed keenly for lifetime batting honors, too. "Irish" ended his career with a .310 average; Bob with a .309!

The Waners played in the same outfield with the Pirates for 13-plus seasons. They compiled the highest lifetime averages of the four families. Paul "Big Poison" Waner hit .333; Lloyd "Little Poison," .316.

Eight times Paul collected 200 hits in a season; four times Lloyd did the same. Overall, Paul amassed 3,152 safeties; Lloyd, 2,459!

Two of the DiMaggio brothers, Joe and Dom, were consistent hitters. The third, Vince, was a journeyman long-ball threat. Joe's lifetime mark was .325. Dom's career average (.298) fell just two points shy of .300.

The two best center fielders of their time, Joe and Dom, were always competing for the pennant. Three times during their careers, the Red Sox finished second to the pennant-winning Yankees; and three times the Bosox wound up third to the flag-winning Yankees. Once the Pinstripers ended up third behind the pace-setting Red Sox and second-place Tigers.

All three of the Alou brothers, Matty, Felipe, and Jesus, were good contact hitters. Matty, the best of the three, batted .307 career-wise. Felipe and Jesus flirted with .280.

But Matty and Felipe Alou did something that no other two brothers have ever done: they finished one-two in a batting race.

In 1966 Matty, who played with the Pirates, led the league with a .342 average; Felipe, who performed for the Braves, finished the runner-up with a mark of .327!

Champions but No Clemency

Chances are pretty good if a seasoned follower of baseball were asked, "What black player in the National League hit for the highest average in a single season?" he would probably respond with one of the following: Willie Mays, Hank Aaron, Roberto Clemente, Ralph Garr, or Jackie Robinson.

But if he didn't say Rico Carty, he would be wrong. In 1970 Carty hit .366 for the Atlanta Braves.

If the same baseball fan were asked, "What black player who spent ten-years-or-more in the major leagues retired with the highest average?" he would probably reply, "Jackie Robinson."

And he would be wrong again. Robinson retired with a lifetime average of .311 but Roberto Clemente's final average was .317!

Breaking in with a Bang

What do Elston Howard and Gene Tenace have in common?

Well, both played behind the plate, hit from the right-hand side, and performed on world championship teams. But many players caught, hit right-handed, and competed for champions.

Howard and Tenace stand out because both hit home runs in their first World Series at-bats. In fact, Tenace set a record when he clouted home runs in his first *two* official appearances in World Series play!

Going into post-season play, both Howard and Tenace were part-time players. Neither had as many as 300 official at-bats. But Howard, a rookie, slammed a Don Newcombe offering into the left field stands on September 28, 1955; and Tenace, a fourth-year man, clubbed a Gary Nolan serve into the left field stands on October 14, 1972.

Overall, Howard had just a mediocre World Series (5-26)

while Tenace (8-23) tore the cover off the ball. The A's catcher-first baseman slugged four home runs and drove home nine runs. The only other players who have hit four home runs in one World Series were Lou Gehrig, Babe Ruth, Hank Bauer, and Duke Snider (twice). Reggie Jackson, of course, hit five.

That's pretty good company for a part-time player!

The Classic Consistency of Clemente

Roberto Clemente played in the shadows of Hank Aaron and Willie Mays during his National League career. That statement won't surprise many followers of the Senior Circuit. But it might surprise some of those same National League aficionados to read that Clemente also played in the shadow of Joe DiMaggio and Hank Bauer, two American League stars.

How? Well, "The Yankee Clipper" hit safely in 56 consecutive games to set a major league regular season record; and "Hammering Hank" connected safely in 17 straight World Series games to set a major league post-season mark. Clemente had a streak of his own: he hit safely in 14 consecutive World Series games.

On the surface Clemente's feat pales when it is set beside the accomplishments of DiMaggio and Bauer. But beneath the surface it sparkles.

Why? Well, DiMaggio's streak took place midway through a career of 1,736 regular season games; and Bauer's toward the end of a career of 53 World Series games. Al Smith and Jim Bagby of the Indians eventually stopped DiMaggio's streak, and Warren Spahn of the Braves finally ended Bauer's.

What is remarkable about Clemente's streak is that he played in *only* 14 World Series games. No pitcher has broken his skein. Not yet! Not ever!

An Average Hitter

Rod Carew, who has won six batting titles for the Twins, won the 1972 hitting crown in a way unlike any other major league champ.

He hit .318, which is low for him; and he hit no home runs, which is low for anyone.

Carew thereby became the only player who has won a batting championship without hitting a home run!

To Athletes Dying Young

Many baseball players die young. Four such were Ed Delahanty, Ross Youngs, Lou Gehrig, and Roberto Clemente.

Delahanty, removed from a train near Niagara Falls early in 1903 because of bad behavior, plunged from the Niagara Falls Bridge to his death into the rapids below after a scuffle with a trestleman who tried to warn him of his impending fate. A .346 lifetime hitter, Delahanty was the second man to hit four home runs in one game and the only man to win batting titles in both leagues. "Big Ed" was 36 when he died. But the year before his death, in 1902, he hit .376 to win the batting title with the Senators.

From 1917-1926 Youngs was an outstanding outfielder for John McGraw's Giants. At the age of 30 he died of a kidney ailment. The year before he died he hit .306 for the Giants. In fact, in nine of his ten major league seasons he hit better than .300.

Gehrig, "The Iron Horse," who set an unbelievable endurance record by playing in 2,130 consecutive games, was hit with a crippling disease at the age of 36 and died two years later. The year before he was forced into retirement, he knocked in 100 runs for the 11th time in his career. He left behind him a lifetime batting average of .340 and 493 home runs.

Clemente, who was still terrorizing opposing pitchers at the age of 38, died when his plane, loaded with supplies for the relief of refugees from the Nicaraguan earthquake, crashed.

The preceding baseball year, he had joined the ranks of baseball's immortal hitters when he collected his 3,000th hit. In fact, the last hit of his major league career, off Jon Matlack of the Mets, won his 3,000th!

61

Rich's Era

Most baseball people associate Richie Allen with the National League. But he had more success in his three years in the American League than he did in 11 seasons in the Senior Circuit.

In his three seasons with the White Sox (1972-74), the .293 lifetime hitter won two home run titles — his only ones — and one RBI crown—his only one. He also hit higher than .300 in all three seasons and averaged .308 overall!

The Three Braves

Many times two players on the same team have hit 40-or-more home runs in the same season, but only once have three players on the same team done it: Davy Johnson, Darrell Evans, and Hank Aaron of the Braves in 1973.

For Aaron it was the eighth time he had hit 40 home runs in a season. For Johnson and Evans it was the first—and only—time they hit 40.

But Johnson set a record which would stand a long time: he hit more home runs (43) in 1973 than any other major league second baseman ever hit in a single season. The former record of 42 was held by Rogers Hornsby of the Cardinals.

"The Rajah's" record had stood for 51 years!

Schmidt: Home-Run King but No All Star

Mike Schmidt of the Phillies, although he won the home run title for three consecutive years (1974-76), has not been accorded the recognition that a slugger of his stature usually commands.

Since 1933, when the All Star Game was initiated, only three major leaguers have won the home run title three years in a row: Mel Ott, Ralph Kiner, and Harmon Killebrew. Ott from 1936-38, Kiner from 1946-52, and Killebrew from 1962-64.

Ott, Kiner, and Killebrew, during the time they were reeling off consecutive home run titles, were permanent fixtures in the All Star Game's starting line-up. On the other hand, Schmidt has never started an All Star Game!

In his three seasons with the White Sox, Richie Allen won two home-run titles and one RBI crown.

The Reds' MVP Men

When the Cincinnati Reds win personal honors, they win them in bunches!

Overall, eight Reds have won a total of ten MVP awards: Ernie Lombardi, Bucky Walters, Frank McCormick, Frank Robinson, Johnny Bench, Pete Rose, Joe Morgan, and George Foster.

Lombardi, the catcher, won the first Reds' MVP Award in 1938. Bucky Walters, the pitcher, and Frank McCormick, the first baseman, copped the titles during the succeeding two years. In 1939 the Reds won the pennant; in 1940 they won the pennant and World Series.

In the past eight years Reds' players have won six MVP awards. Johnny Bench received the honor in 1970 and 1972, Pete Rose in 1973, Joe Morgan in both 1975 and 1976, and George Foster in 1977. The Reds won pennants in 1970 and 1972, a division title in 1973, and world championships in 1975 and 1976,

In 1961 Robinson won an isolated award. The Reds copped the pennant that year, too. Robinson, of course, would be an exception to any rule. He was the only player who has won MVP awards in both leagues!

Endurance and Energy

Stan Musial and Billy Williams have several things in common.

First, they have both been batting champions. Musial won seven hitting titles with the Cardinals; Williams, one with the Cubs.

They also set streaks for consecutive games played. Musial held the National League record until Williams set a new mark of 1,117 games.

They both hit the long ball, too. Musial poled 475 home runs while Williams hit 426 circuit clouts. They are two of 17 players who have hit 400-or-more home runs in their careers.

But they are the *only* two of the 17 who have failed to win a home run title!

Clutch Hitters in a Pinch

The four most successful pinch-hitters in major league history are Tommy Davis, Frenchy Bordagaray, Frank Baumholtz, and Red Schoendienst. All hit better than .300 in substitute roles.

In a 17-year career Davis hit a .313 average in single-shot appearances. Overall, he pinch-hit safely 55 times in 176 tries. His best single-season performance was in 1971, when he batted .464 for Oakland. He made 13 hits in 28 pinch-hit appearances.

In an 11-year career Bordagaray stung the ball at a .312 clip when he came off the bench. His best year as pinch-hitter was in 1938 when he hit .465 for the Cardinals in a substitute role. He hit safely 20 times in 43 pinch-hit appearances.

In a ten-year career Baumholtz ripped the ball at a .307 pace when he stepped to the plate as a pinch-hitter. His best year as a substitute batter was 1955 when he hit .405 for the Cubs. He got 15 safeties in 37 pinch-hit at-bats.

In a 19-year career Schoendienst met the ball for a .303 average in late-game appearances. His best year as a substitute batter was 1961 when he hit .333 as a pinch-hitter. He connected safely 16 times in 48 times at-bats. David, Bordagaray, Baumholtz, and Schoendienst all hit better in pinch-hitting appearances than in regular game roles. As regulars they hit .295, .283, .290, and .289!

Hitters who Made Their Point

What's the difference between batting .300 and .299? One point? Don't believe it.

Wally Berger, Ethan Allen, Enos Slaughter, and Billy Goodman all ended up their careers with flat .300 averages, and they're happy in retirement. Minnie Minoso finished his career with a .299 mark, and he's not.

In fact, at the age of 57, Bill Veeck, the owner of the White Sox, activated him during the last month of the 1976 season so that the player-coach might have a chance to raise his lifetime average to .300.

That's the difference between batting .300 and .299!

Nettled Memories

Graig Nettles of the Yankees, who won the American League home run title in 1976, has hit more home runs than any other third baseman in the Bronx Bombers' history — 134. Overall, with the Twins, the Indians, and the Yankees, he has hit .217.

Clete Boyer held the former Yankee mark with 95.

Those figures are surprisingly low for a Yankees' position. Another surprise is that Nettles was the first Yankees' home run champion since Roger Maris hit his record 61 homers in 1961.

In the 41 years before 1961, Yankees' batters won a total of 22 home run crowns, an average of better than one every two years!

The .375 Hitter: A Dying Breed

Batters have hit .375-or-better a total of 69 times.

Ty Cobb leads both the American League and the major leagues with 11 averages that were in that range. Rogers Hornsby leads the National League with seven averages that were in that range.

The last American League player who hit .375-or-over was Rod Carew, who batted .388 in 1977. The last National League player who hit .375-or-over was Stan Musial. He batted .376 in 1948!

Two Tough Twins

Tony Oliva and Rod Carew of the Twins have had a lock on the American League batting championship for the past 14 years. Oliva has won the title three times; Carew, six.

Oliva won his batting titles in 1964, 1965, and 1971. Carew copped his in 1969, in 1972-75, and in 1977. He was the second player in the history of the American League to win four consecutive batting crowns. Only Ty Cobb, who won nine consecutive championships (1907-15), won four-or-more titles, too.

In the National League Honus Wagner won four straight from 1906-09, and Rogers Hornsby won six in a row from 1920-25.

Players before Their Time

Everything in baseball is relative.

Take batting. There have been five players who hit .392-or-better in a single season and didn't win the batting championship. On the other hand, there have been five players who hit .318-or-less in a single season and did win it.

In 1911 Joe Jackson batted .408 but he finished second to Ty Cobb, who hit .420. Cobb got burned in 1922 when his .401 ended up second to George Sisler's .420. Babe Ruth hit a career high of .393 in 1923, but Harry Heilmann batted .403. In 1927 Al Simmons batted a ripe .392, but Heilmann hit .398. Billy Herman got snakebitten in 1930 when he hit .393, for Bill Terry batted .401 the same year.

On the other hand, the following players won batting averages with relatively anemic marks: Rod Carew, .318 (1972); Frank Robinson, .316 (1966); George Stirnweiss, .309 (1945); Elmer Flick, .306 (1905); and Carl Yastrzemski, .301 (1968).

That's how relative the game is. A player can hit .408 one year and not win the batting title, yet hit .301 the following year and win it.

The Royal Choice

Jackie Robinson, the first black to play in the major leagues, distinguished himself on the very first day he crossed the base lines of a white diamond.

No, it wasn't with Brooklyn, where he hit .311, batted 137 home runs, and stole 197 bases en route to an invitation to the Hall of Fame. It was with Montreal, where he first broke into professional baseball with the Royals, who were the Dodgers' Triple-A farm team in the International League.

On the opening day of the 1946 season, in Jersey City's Roosevelt Stadium, he hit a homer and two singles, stole two bases, and scored four runs as the Royals defeated the Giants 14-1!

Four Is a Lucky Number

Willie McCovey and Lou Gehrig, believe it or not, have a lot of things in common.

Gehrig, of course, was the superior hitter. "The Iron Horse" holds a commanding edge in the lifetime batting department— .340 to McCovey's .274.

But in the slugging department they match up pretty evenly. Gehrig won two home-run crowns outright. McCovey won two home-run crowns outright. Gehrig, on another occasion, tied for the home-run lead. So did McCovey.

Gehrig holds the major league lead and the American League high with 23 grand slams. McCovey holds the National League high with 18 grand slams.

And, after the 1977 season, both had hit 493 lifetime homers.

They even looked alike in the batting box. Both batted from the left-hand side of the plate, and both wore the same number on their backs.

Gehrig wore Number 4; McCovey, Number 44!

Canada's Fair-Haired Boy

Hitting .279, cracking 19 home runs, and driving home 64 runs would be considered a good season for just about any major leaguer. But performing those feats in one's 20th season, as Ron Fairly did for the expansion Toronto Blue Jays last year, has to be considered an extraordinary feat for the Canadian ballplayer.

Of course Fairly has had an extraordinary career, so it comes as no great surprise that he turned in the season he did.

In his first 12 seasons in the big leagues, with the Los Angeles Dodgers, he had one .300 season, .322 in 1961, and a .300 average for four World Series. Then he moved to Montreal, where he averaged .273 and 15 home runs per season for five years.

After single seasons with the Cardinals—for whom he batted .301—and the A's, he was picked up in the expansion draft by the Blue Jays. In 1977, with Toronto, he upped his career totals to .268 (batting average) and 205 (home runs).

Fairly has been the only ballplayer who has performed with both Canadian franchises, the Blue Jays and the Expos. If he lasts another three years—and present indications are that he will—he'll join a very select group of players (since 1939) who have performed during four different decades in the major leagues: Ted Williams, Mickey Vernon, Early Wynn, and Minnie Minoso.

That's fairly good company!

Catfish Hunter is the most celebrated pitcher of modern times.

THE PITCHERS

Young's True Test

If Denton Cy "True" Young wasn't the best pitcher who ever lived — a check of the records indicates that he might have been — he was certainly the most durable moundsman who ever threw a baseball!

Young's pitching feats were truly amazing. Over a 22-year career with the Indians, Cardinals, and Red Sox, he won 511 games. During that same stretch he lost 313 contests. Both totals rank as the all-time high for the number of games won and lost. What is even more astounding about these figures, however, is that he pitched 824 games to a decision. That is eight games more than the number of contests that he started — 816! (He worked 90 games in relief, too.)

Of the 816 games he started, the all-time high, he completed 750 of them, also the all-time high. His completion mark was an incredible 92 percent, another all-time high!

He performed other extraordinary exploits, too. For example, he won 20-or-more games 14 times, he won 30-or-more games five times, and he pitched three no-hitters, one of which was a perfect game.

But one has to compare his completion percentage with other greats of the game to realize how truly good he was. Lefty Grove, one of the all-time greats, completed 300 of 456 starts for a percentage of 66; Whitey Ford, the best lefthander in the

American League since Grove, finished 156 of 438 starts for a mark of 36 per cent; and Catfish Hunter, the most celebrated pitcher of modern times, has gone the distance in 175 of 437 starts for an average of 40 percent!

McGinnity: The Real Iron Man

Joe McGinnity, "The Iron Man," was well named. First, he actually did once work in an iron foundry. Second, he made his reputation by involving himself in endurance feats.

In his first eight years in the majors, he won 20-or-more games in each season. In fact, in 1903 and 1904 for the Giants, he won 32 and 33 games. The phenomenal righthander led the league in starts six times; wins and innings pitched, four times; winning percentage and games completed, two times; and earned run average, one time.

Lifetime, McGinnity posted a 2.66 ERA. In 1903 he started 48 games, the third highest number in history. Twice he pitched more than 400 innings in a season: 1903 (434) and 1904 (408). Only one other National League pitcher has thrown 400 innings in a season. Vic Willis of the Braves hurled 410 innings in 1902. In 1903 McGinnity completed 44 games, the second highest total in National League history. (Willis completed 45 in 1902.) But perhaps his most impressive statistic is his record of finishing 314 of 381 lifetime starts for a completion ratio of 82 percent.

In 1900 while he was with the Dodgers, he won five games in six days. Later with the Giants he once won ten games in 12 days. But in 1903 "The Iron Man" outdid himself. In August of that year, he pitched both ends of a doubleheader three times; and he won both ends of a doubleheader three times.

He pitched all of the games in less than two hours!

Never on a Sunday

Christy Mathewson, the great pitcher for the Giants, never pitched a major league game on a Sunday; Branch Rickey, the great front office man for the Cardinals, Dodgers, and Pirates, never managed a game on a Sunday!

"Big Six" did not even dress in uniform, and "The Mahatma" never went near the ballpark nor watched a game.

Mathewson, according to Fred Snodgrass, a teammate with the Giants, was not an over-religious type of person. But he started playing baseball with the belief that professional sports should not be played on Sunday, and he never changed. Rickey claimed he had promised his mother he would never go near a ballpark on a Sunday, and he kept his promise.

That promise almost cost him his major league career. In 1903 he signed with the Reds. But he never played with Cincinnati because he refused to take the field on Sunday. So he was dropped. In 1905-06 he caught for the Browns. The following year, he was a part-time player with the Highlanders; and in 1914, after seven years of inactivity, he wound up his playing career with the Browns.

But he managed the Browns for ten years (1913-15 and 1919-25). During that time he never managed his club on a Sunday. Jimmy Austin, his third baseman, would substitute-manage for him.

In those days Sunday ball was not played in the East. But it was played in Chicago, Cincinnati, and St. Louis. So Rickey did not miss too many Sundays while he was on the road, but he did miss a lot of games when his club was at home.

Mathewson, on the other hand, didn't miss any games at home. But he did miss pitching turns when the Giants played the host Cubs, Reds, or Cardinals.

Rickey's absence did not cost the Browns any pennants. His highest finish with the Browns was third place. His overall winning percentage was a sub-average .473. But Matty's absence from the line-up could have cost the Giants two pennants. In 1906 the Giants finished three games behind the pennant-winning Cubs; in 1908 the Giants lost out to the Cubs by one game.

Could Mathewson's presence on a Sunday have made the

difference during those years? Well, the Cubs, of course, played Sunday games at home. There were times when manager John McGraw would dearly have liked Matty's presence on one of those Sundays. But no one ever heard the Cubs complain about the absence of "Big Six"!

Ed Walsh's One-Man Show

Never in the history of the national pastime has one pitcher done so much, with so little support, to carry his team to the brink of victory than Ed Walsh of the White Sox did in 1908.

"Big Ed" won the phenomenal total of 40 games—one short of Jack Chesbro's all-time record of 41—and he lost only 15 while capturing the pitching championship with a winning percentage of .727. The winning percentage was indeed phenomenal, for the White Sox batted an incredibly low .224, the lowest in the league. The entire team hit only three home runs, the fewest a big league team had hit since 1900. Walsh tied for the club home run high, with one. To make it worse, the team's slugging percentage was a paltry .271, the lowest average, by 20 points, in the American League.

But Walsh kept the White Sox in the pennant race. Going into the last game of the season, the White Sox and Indians were separated from the league-leading Tigers by only half a game.

The big righthander led the league in shutouts, 12; strikeouts, 269; ERA, 1.42; games, 66; starts, 49; completions, 42; and innings, 464, (a major league record for one season).

Fielder Jones, the Sox's manager, pitched his meal ticket in seven of the team's last nine games. In two of those games Walsh pitched and won a doubleheader against the Red Sox. In one of those games he lost 1-0 to Addie Joss of the Indians, who pitched the second perfect game of the twentieth century. Walsh struck out 15 batters (a club record that stood until 1954) and limited the Indians to four singles. Joe Birmingham, who scored the winning run, reached first on an error, stole two bases, and scored on a passed ball.

The last National League player to hit .375 or over was Stan Musial. He batted .376 in 1948.

The showdown came on October 6, the final day of the season. The Indians, though only half a game out of first place, had been eliminated from contention by percentage points. So, when the Tigers and White Sox took the field at Comiskey Park, it was winner-take-all. But in the biggest game of the year the White Sox had to go with Doc White, an 18-game winner, because Walsh had simply pitched himself out.

White was not sharp, though, and he gave up three hits in one-third of an inning. Jones panicked and called for Walsh, who had not even had a chance to warm up. Exhausted and unprepared, Walsh was raked for six hits in three and two thirds innings; and the Tigers went on to win the game, 7-0.

To add insult to injury, Walsh was charged with the loss. Under the present rules, White would have been charged with the first three runs and subsequently the loss. But the official scorer must have thought that Walsh, who had been performing miracles all season long, was not entitled to an off-day.

But a win by Walsh on that day sure would have changed history, and students of the game would recall the year 1908 not only as the year of "Merkle's Boner" but also as the year of "Big Ed" Walsh's one-man show, the greatest single-season, one-man pitching show that has ever been recorded!

Reulbach and Grove: Blue Chip Pitchers

Ed Reulbach of the Cubs and Lefty Grove of the Athletics were the only two pitchers who have won their league's winning percentage title three straight years.

Reulbach paced the Cubs with winning percentage marks of .833, .810, and .774 in 1906, 1907, and 1908. Grove led the A's with winning percentage averages of .769, .848, and .886 in 1929, 1930, and 1931.

Grove was by far the better pitcher. He won 300 games while Reulbach won 185. Eight times Grove won 20-or-more games in a season; three times Reulbach amassed 20-or-more victories in a year.

But Reulbach, in 1908, accomplished something which neither Grove nor any other pitcher in the history of the game has ever achieved: he pitched shutouts in both ends of a double-header.

Coincidentally, the Cubs won three pennants and two world championships while Reulbach was leading the league in winning percentage. And the A's won three pennants and two world championships while Grove was pacing the American League in winning percentage!

The Imperfect Perfect Pitcher

Had Addie Joss of the Indians (1902-10) been blessed with good health, he might have become one of the greatest pitchers of all time. As it is, he left an incredible nine-year record behind him.

Four times Joss won 20-or-more games. Five times he posted ERAs of less than 2.00. His highest ERA for one season was 2.77. His lifetime ERA was 1.88, which is second to Ed Walsh's all-time low of 1.82.

Twice in his brief career he pitched no-hitters. The first one was a perfect game against the White Sox in 1908. It was the second perfect game in the history of modern baseball.

But his health was not good. In 1910, his final season, he became ill. The following season he died — at 31.

Matty's Mastery

For 14 years Christy Mathewson was the most consistent winner ever to pitch.

From 1901-14 he won a total of 355 games, an average of 25 per season. Thirteen times during that period he won 20 games in a season. Warren Spahn was the only pitcher who has duplicated this feat. (Cy Young surpassed it with 14 20-game sessions.) But Spahn never won more than 23 games in one season. Mathewson won more than 30 games in a season three times. In fact, from 1903-08, he averaged 29 wins per season.

But the incredible time of Mathewson's career was between 1903 and 1914, a period of 12 *consecutive* years, when he won more than 20 games in each season. The closest that any other pitcher has come to duplicating that achievement was Walter Johnson, who won 20 games in ten consecutive seasons to set an American League record!

The Big Train's Express Performance

Walter Johnson, "The Big Train," was the shutout king of major league baseball.

The Senators' righthander, who completed 532 of 666 starts for a route-going percentage of 80 per cent, won 416 games, the second highest number of wins in the history of the game.

One out of every four of those wins was a shutout. He pitched 112 shutouts. In his 21-year career he pitched 112 shutouts. Grover Alexander ranks second on the all-time list with 88 shutouts, which are 24 shy of Johnson's total.

In fact, Johnson pitched in 65 games in which only one run was scored. He won 38 and he lost 27. In 20 of those 27 losses, he allowed four-or-less hits!

Bender's Route

Chief Bender of the Athletics, who had a career record of 208-127, had a habit of finishing whatever he started.

In his 16-year career he completed 257 of 335 starts for a 77 percent completion rate. But he outdid himself in World Series play. Ten times he started a World Series game, and nine times he completed it.

Bender, who was 6-4 in World Series play, completed the first nine games he started against National League opponents!

One Rube of a Pitcher

Consistency has been the trademark of great players. Rube Marquard, Walter Johnson, Joe Wood, Lefty Grove, Schoolboy

Rowe, and Carl Hubbell were six consistent pitchers who left great records behind them. So consistent were they that they set major league records for consecutive wins in one season.

The year 1912 was an especially good one for pitchers. In that year major league, National League, and American League records for pitchers were established.

Marquard, 27-11 for the Giants that year, reeled off 20 wins in a row to set both a major league and a National League record. Over the past 65 years his winning streak has not been seriously challenged.

In the same year the Senators' Walter Johnson, who finished the season with a 32-12 count, won 16 straight games to set an American League mark that has not been broken. Later in the season Wood, 34-5 for the Red Sox, put 13 consecutive wins together. Sports editors throughout the East insisted Johnson should have a chance to defend his record. So the Red Sox and Senators matched Wood and Johnson before an overflow crowd at Fenway Park. The game ended just about the way one might have expected — 1-0; with Wood on the winning end. The Boston righthander went on to win two more games and tie Johnson's mark.

Lefty Grove of the Athletics (31-4) strung 16 straight wins together in 1931, too, as did Schoolboy Rowe of the Tigers (24-8) in 1934. Grove's string came to an end when a substitute outfielder, Jim Moore, misjudged a fly ball that allowed the Browns to win 1-0. Grove bitterly contends that had Al Simmons, the regular leftfielder, been in the lineup he would not only have won the game, but would also have extended the major league record to 24 consecutive wins. He's got a solid argument: after that heartbreaking loss, Grove reeled off seven straight wins.

Somebody actually did win 24 consecutive games — Carl Hubbell. But he did it in two years (1936-37) not one!

Double No-Hitter

On May 2, 1917, Fred Toney of the Reds and Jim "Hippo" Vaughn of the Cubs hooked up in what has most probably been the best pitchers' duel of all time: for nine full innings both of them pitched no-hitters.

The only double no-hitter of all time was broken up in the tenth inning when the Reds scored a run on two hits and won the game, 1-0. Toney held the Cubs hitless in the tenth to pitch a ten-inning no-hitter.

The winning run was scored on an infield hit to third base by an outfielder for the Reds—Jim Thorpe!

The Pitcher who Upstaged the Babe

Babe Ruth was such a remarkable player that he even got his name into the record book in a game in which he failed to retire one single batter in a starting role.

On June 23, 1917, Washington's lead-off batter, Ray Morgan, walked off a full count. The incensed Babe, who thought that he had picked up the corner of the plate, boiled blasphemously, and the umpire cooled him off with an early shower. Ernie Shore (63-42) came on in relief; and, after Morgan was erased on an attempted steal, he retired 26 consecutive batters to record the third perfect game in modern history.

What makes Shore's feat unique, though, is the fact that it was the only perfect game that has ever been thrown by a relief pitcher!

The Coveleskis' 20-Game Beat

Gaylord and Jim Perry have been the most successful pitching brothers in baseball's history. They have won a total of 461 games — Gaylord 246, Jim 215. But Stan and Harry Coveleski performed feats that even the Perry brothers haven't matched.

Stan, who compiled a 217-141 lifetime record, between 1917 and 1921 reeled off five consecutive 20 game seasons for the Indians. In the 1920 World Series he won three games against the Dodgers; and the Tribe won its first world's title. Traded to the Senators in 1925, he pitched Washington to its second pennant in as many years with a record of 20-5.

Harry, who registered an 81-57 career mark, won 66 of his lifetime wins in three seasons. He won 20 games for the Tigers in each season from 1914-16. In 1914 he won 21 games; in 1915, 23; and in 1916, 22.

Earlier in his career Harry earned the nickname of "The Giant Killer" when he defeated the McGrawmen three times in a five-game series for the Phillies. But the Giants eventually "drummed" him out of the league after they found out his girl had run off with a drum major. The Giants' mock beating of drums on their dugout steps affected Harry's composure. But by the time he got to the American League, he had regained control. In his first three seasons with the Tigers, he enjoyed 20 game seasons.

Overall, the Coveleski brothers racked up a total of eight 20-game seasons, the most of any pitching brothers. The Perrys, for example, have won 20 games a total of six times!

Alexander the Great

Grover "Pete" Alexander, who blanked his opponents 88 times during his 20-year National League career, was the shutout artist of all senior circuit pitchers.

Seven times during his career he led the league in shutouts. Three times he shut out every team in the league. That's a major league record.

But Alexander was no stranger to records. He set a record when he won 20-or-more games in his first seven years in the major leagues. In his first four years he ended up in the 20-win column every season; in his fifth to seventh seasons he wound up in the 30-win column every year. If World War I had not interrupted his torrid start, he might have continued *ad infinitum*. When he returned from the service, he established himself as one of the best pitchers in the National League. But he was no longer the *great* pitcher he had been.

Yet he remains the greatest shutout artist in the history of the National League. In 1916 he pitched 16 shutouts, the major league high for the total of blankings in one season; in 1921 he hurled three whitewashes, the major league low for the most shutouts in one year!

The Big Four

Two pitching staffs in the history of baseball have had four 20-game winners on it: the 1920 White Sox and the 1971 Orioles. But only one of the two won the pennant.

Dave McNally (21-5), Pat Dobson (20-8), Mike Cuellar (20-9), and Jim Palmer (20-9) were the 20-game winners for the 1971 Orioles, who distanced the Tigers by 12 games in the Eastern Division and swept the A's in three games in the playoffs. The Birds then lost to the Pirates in the World Series four games to three.

Red Faber (23-13), Lefty Williams (22-14), Dickie Kerr (21-9), and Ed Cicotte (21-10) were the 20-game winners for the 1920 White Sox, who went down to the wire with the Indians.

But, in the waning days of the season, there were rumors concerning a conspiracy on the part of eight White Sox' players to fix the 1919 World Series.

The White Sox then faded and lost the pennant by two games. But they lost more than a pennant: they lost a franchise. The eight players were permanently barred from professional baseball. And the White Sox did not win another pennant for 39 years!

Sad Sam's Secret

When the Reds swept the Yankees in the 1976 World Series, it seemed as though the New York pitchers had never practiced a pick-off play in their lives. But perhaps they were just stealing a page from the book of a former Yankee great, Sam Jones.

"Sad Sam," who won 229 games for five American League teams, at one point in his career did not throw to first base for five years. He didn't believe in it. He said it only shortened a pitcher's career.

Jones (1914-35) pitched 22 *consecutive* years in the American

Willie McCovey (above) and Lou Gehrig have a lot in common. For one, after the 1971 season, both had hit 493 lifetime homers.

League. That's a league record for pitchers. Maybe he knew what he was talking about!

Pennock: The Perfect Knight

Herb Pennock, who pitched for the Athletics, Red Sox, and Yankees, had the most impressive mound record in World Series history.

That's saying a lot.

Allie Reynolds of the Yankees had seven wins and four saves, but he lost two games. Red Ruffing of the Yankees and Bob Gibson of the Cardinals each won seven games, but they lost two contests, too. And Lefty Gomez of the Yankees had a perfect 6-0 mound mark.

But Pennock, "The Knight of Kennett Square," had a perfect 5-0 record; and in five relief spots, he saved three games. So in eight World Series decisions he played a positive part in all eight games!

Zachary's Moments to Remember

Tom Zachary, who pitched for seven major league teams, won 185 games. But he is best remembered for one pitch that he threw: the ball Babe Ruth hit for his 60th home run in 1927.

Some of Zachary's noteworthy achievements have gone relatively unnoticed, though. In World Series play, with the Senators in 1924 and 1925 and the Yankees in 1928, he posted a record of 3-0.

In 1929, two years after his historic pitch, he turned in a 12-0 record for the Yankees—the most victories any pitcher has ever recorded in one season without tasting defeat!

Good Hitting Pitchers

What did Lefty O'Doul, Ted Williams, Babe Ruth, George Sisler, Stan Musial, Honus Wagner, Jimmy Foxx, Sam Rice, and Rube Bressler have in common?

They were all .300 lifetime hitters? Well, yes, they were. But there was something else.

Give up? Well, they were all pitchers at one time or another. Eight of the nine pitched in the majors: O'Doul, Williams, Ruth, Sisler, Wagner, Foxx, Rice, and Bressler.

O'Doul, who hit .349 had a 1-3 record with the Yankees and the Red Sox. In 34 games of relief, he posted a 4.87 ERA.

Williams, who batted .344, gave up one run in two innings of relief in a 1940 game.

Ruth, of course, was a bona fide major league pitcher. He chalked up a 94-46 record with a 2.28 ERA for a winning percentage of .671. If he had continued to pitch, he undoubtedly would have become one of the all-time mound greats. But he switched to the outfield and became one of the all-time great outfielders. He batted .342 lifetime.

Sisler, who hit .340, appeared on the mound in seven different seasons. Overall he posted a 5-6 record with a 2.35 ERA.

Wagner pitched eight and one third innings in 1900 and 1902. He gave up eight hits but didn't yield any runs. "The Flying Dutchman's" forte was hitting, though. He batted .329 and won eight batting titles.

Foxx turned to the mound late in his career. In brief appearances with the Red Sox and the Phillies, he registered a 1-0 mark. In twenty two and two third innings he posted a 1.52 ERA. As a batter he hit .325.

Rice, who hit .322, had a 1-1 record in 1915 and 1916. In nine games he had one route-going performance and a 2.52 ERA.

Bressler, who batted .301, pitched seven years in the big leagues. He recorded a 14-22 mark with the Athletics and a 12-7 log with the Reds. In starts he pitched three shutouts, and in relief he posted an 8-6 mark.

Musial never pitched an inning in the majors. He was a promising pitcher with Columbus in the American Association, but diving for a catch one day, he hurt his pitching shoulder. So he concentrated on the outfield.

"The Man's" lifetime average was .331—the same mark as the combined averages of all nine players who were once pitchers but who had the good foresight to give up the mound for a regular position and four official at-bats per day at the plate !

Pitchers with Greener Pastures

Competition quite often brings out the best in pitchers—take the careers of Rube Bressler and Lefty O'Doul as examples.

In 1914, when Bressler came to the majors with the Athletics, he had to earn a spot on a mound staff that included pitchers Eddie Plank, Chief Bender, Herb Pennock, Bullet Joe Bush, Jack Coombs, and Bob Shawkey. Plank, Bender, and Pennock are in the Hall of Fame; Bush and Shawkey each won 196 games; and Coombs once won 30 games in a season 13 shutout games in another—an American League record.

When O'Doul tried to break in with the Yankees (from 1919-22), he had to earn a spot on a mound staff that included pitchers Carl Mays, Sam Jones, Bush, Shawkey, and Pennock. Mays, Jones, and Pennock won 200 games; Bush and Shawkey, 196.

So in time, Bressler, who ended up with a career pitching record of 26-31, and O'Doul, who finished with a career mound record of 1-1, switched to the outfield. And with great success!

Five times Bressler hit .300. From 1924-26 with the Reds, Bressler averaged .351 with the bat. In 1926 he hit .357, the highest batting average in the National League. Career-wise, he hit .301.

O'Doul's lifetime average was a sensational .349. In 1929 he won the National League batting title while he was with the Phillies, with a mark of .398. One additional hit for O'Doul in 1929 would have enabled him to join a select group of eight hitters who have batted .400. The following year, O'Doul batted .383. The Phillies must have thought he was slipping, because they traded him to the Dodgers, with whom he won a batting title in 1932, with an average of .368.

Bressler and O'Doul were two players who found it was easier to stay in the major leagues by hitting against pitchers rather than pitching against hitters!

Grove's ERA Ups and Downs

Twenty-three pitchers have posted lifetime ERAs of 2.49-or-less.

But Lefty Grove, a 300-game winner for the Athletics and the Red Sox, was not one of them. In fact, Grove's lifetime ERA was a relatively high 3.06. He did things in the ERA column that no other pitcher has ever done, though. Overall, he won eight ERA titles; a record. He won four of them with the A's and four of them with the Red Sox. The only other pitcher who has won multiple ERA titles with more than one team was Grover Alexander, who won three championships with the Phillies and two with the Cubs.

But the ERA feats for which Grove is best remembered happened in the late 1920s and early 1930s. From 1929-32 he won four consecutive ERA titles. To appreciate that performance properly, one should have a basis of comparison: Cy Young, who won a record 511 games during his career, copped only two ERA crowns in 22 years!

The Mound's Super Sluggers

Wes Ferrell, Bob Lemon, Red Ruffing, and Warren Spahn were great pitchers. They were great sluggers, too. For pitchers, that is.

Ferrell holds the all-time home run lead for pitchers with 38 four-base blows; Lemon, second place with 37; Ruffing, third place with 36; and Spahn, fourth place with 35.

When one looks at the records of pitchers who have hit home runs in consecutive seasons, though, the order reverses itself.

It reads: Spahn, 17; Ruffing, 16; Lemon, 12; and Ferrell, 8.

Ferrell hit the most home runs in the least number of years. From 1931-36 he belted 34 homers, an average of six per season!

The Designated Hitting Pitcher

Babe Ruth was not the only Red Sox pitcher who later became a great hitter for the Yankees. Red Ruffing was another pinstriper who terrorized opposing American League pitchers.

Ruffing, who won 273 games over a 22-year career with the Red Sox, Yankees, and White Sox, was one of the best hitting-pitchers of all time. Lifetime, he hit .269 and stroked 36 home runs, which ranks third to Wes Ferrell (38) and Bob Lemon (37). In addition he drove home 273 runs, which rates him a follow-up spot to Cy Young's 290.

But it was his consistency which made him the truly remarkable hitter that he was. Eight times during his career, he hit .300. That's a major league record for pitchers. Five of those .300 seasons came during consecutive seasons — 1928-32. That's another major league record for moundsmen. During that span with the Red Sox and the Yankees, he averaged .324. In 1930 he hit a career high of .364.

In between pitching starts Ruffing always kept his favorite bat ready: he pinch-hit safely 58 times to establish another record for pitchers.

Times have changed, but one thing is certain: if Red Ruffing were playing today, he would be the one pitcher in the American League who would *not* give up his turn at bat for a designated hitter!

The Home-Run King of Pitchers' Hill

Wes Ferrell won 20-or-more games six times during a 15-year career with six different clubs and was a slugging pitcher who hit for average.

The big righthander, the younger brother of Rick, caught in the majors for 18 years and hit a total of 38 home runs, the most ever hit by a pitcher. For the Indians, in 1931, he slugged nine circuit clouts, the most any hurler has tagged in one season. Twice (1933 and 1935) he hit seven home runs in one season, the second highest number of home runs triggered by a pitcher in one season. But other pitchers have equalled that total: Don Drysdale (1958 and 1965) and Don Newcombe (1955).

From 1934-36 Wes and Rick Ferrell formed a pitcher-catcher battery with the Red Sox. Wes was an outstanding pitcher (193-128) and Rick was an extraordinary catcher. But they both could handle the bat, too. Rick's lifetime average was .281; Wes's, .280. But Wes was the superior slugger. In 1,176 times at bat he hit 38 home runs; in 6,028 times at bat Rick hit only 28.

Wes hit an average of one home run in every 30 trips to the plate. At that rate, had he batted the 12,364 times that Hank Aaron batted, he would have hit a career total of 413 home runs.

That's not bad for a player whose primary job was to get batters out!

The Dean(s) of Pitchers

Career-wise, Dizzy and Daffy Dean were not the best pair of pitching brothers who ever hurled in the majors—Gaylord and Jim Perry were—but for two seasons (1934-35) there was not a better pitching one-two punch in all of baseball.

In 1934 when "The Gashouse Gang" was at its peak, the Dean brothers led the way. Dizzy won 30 games that season. No other National League pitcher since that time has won 30 games. Daffy, who was a rookie, won 19 games. Between them they won 49 games. No other pair of brothers has ever come close to matching that total for one season.

One year later the Dean brothers were almost as good. Dizzy won 28 games to pace the league in victories for the second consecutive year, and Daffy matched the 19 wins that he had posted in his rookie season. So they won a total of 47 games. No other pair of brothers has come close to matching that total, either.

Then tragedy struck. In 1936 Daffy injured his arm and won only seven more major league games. In 1937 Dizzy injured his arm and won only 16 more major league games.

But during their prime they were brilliant. In two regular seasons they won a total of 96 games. And, in the 1934 World Series, they won two games each to lead the Cardinals to a four-to-three-game victory over the Tigers.

So, in two years, the fabulous Dean brothers won a total of 100 games!

The Goofy All Star

Lefty Gomez, who won 189 games in 13 seasons with the Yankees, owned National League batters.

The Hall of Fame lefty defeated National League teams in World Series play six times. The Senior Circuit never tagged "Goofy" with a loss.

In All Star Game play Gomez defeated the National League three times before they pinned a loss on him in 1938. So, overall, Gomez had a 9-1 record against the National League in World Series and all-star activity.

To show baseball fans how they felt about Gomez's mastery over the National League, the American Leaguers started him in the first three all-star classics. In the first six years of the All Star Game, Gomez started five times for the American League!

King Carl's Reign

Carl Hubbell was one of the few National League pitchers who could beat the American League during the 1930s.

During the Depression the American League won seven of ten World Series and five of seven all-star games. But "King Carl," who reeled off five consecutive 20-game seasons from 1933-37, was not intimidated by the Junior Circuit's sluggers.

He won four of six World Series starts and posted an overall ERA of 1.79. In the 1933 World Series he won both of his decisions against the Senators; in the 1936 and 1937 World Series he split a pair of encounters with the Bronx Bombers in each autumn meeting.

90

The potent Yankees lost only three of 23 World Series games during the 1930s. Hubbell dealt them two of their three losses.

"The Meal Ticket" also turned the tide for the Senior Circuit in the All Star Game. The American League won the first three midsummer dream games. But Hubbell registered the National League's first victory when he picked up a 4-3 win in relief in the 1936 classic.

In the 1936 All Star Game Hubbell pitched three scoreless innings. But "King Carl" was even better in the 1934 All Star Game, which the American League won, 11-7. After a rocky start—Charlie Gehringer singled and Heinie Manush walked—Hubbell settled down and performed one of the greatest feats in the history of all sports: in succession he struck out Babe Ruth, Lou Gehrig, Jimmy Foxx, Al Simmons, and Joe Cronin.

Those five hitters — who are all in the Hall of Fame — had a combined lifetime average of .329!

One Start Too Many

Johnny Allen of the Indians was a percentage pitcher (.654) who in 1937 went to the mound once too often.

Going into the last game of the season, Allen had a perfect 15-0 record. But he lost the final game and ended the season with a winning percentage of .938. At that stage in his career, with six full seasons behind him, he had a career record of 85-30 for a winning percentage of .730.

But that one loss in 1937 changed the course of his future. Over the last seven years of his career, he posted a 57-45 mark for a .559 average.

But his .938 winning percentage in 1937 remains the highest for any American League pitcher with at least 15 decisions. The only pitcher in the majors who recorded a higher percentage was Elroy Face, who won 18 and lost only one in 1959 for a sizzling .947!

The No-Hitter who Lit Up Brooklyn

There have been only four pitchers who have thrown two no-hitters in one year: Johnny Vander Meer, Allie Reynolds, Virgil Trucks, and Nolan Ryan.

Vander Meer's feat is the best remembered. He pitched his no-hitters in succession. On June 11, 1938, he no-hit the Braves. Four days later, June 15, he duplicated his previous performance with a no-hitter against the Dodgers at Ebbetts Field in Brooklyn.

What gave Vander Meer's feat in Brooklyn a twofold historical significance was that that contest was the first night game ever played at Ebbetts Field!

Twenty Game Reversals

Bucky Walters and Paul Derringer, the two mainstays of the Reds' pitching staff during their pennant-winning years in 1939 and 1940, did a 360-degree turn as their pitching careers progressed.

Walters, a three-time 20-game winner, in 1936 turned in an 11-21 record for the Phillies. Several years later Walters won 27 and 22, respectively, for the pennant-winning Reds of 1939-40. He also won 23 games for the third-place Reds in 1944.

Derringer, who also had a checkered major league career, had four 20-game seasons. In 1931 as a rookie, the big righthander won 18 games for the pennant-winning Cardinals. A couple of years later he lost 27 and 21 games for the basement Reds. But the Reds improved and so did Derringer's record. In 1935 he won 22 games for a sixth-place team, and in 1938 he won 21 for a fourth-place club. In 1939 and 1940 the Reds won pennants, and during those two years he turned in records of 25-7 and 20-12 respectively.

So Walters and Derringer rebounded from early setbacks in their careers to become two of the best righthanders in the

National League. In 1939 and 1940, counting the World Series, they won a combined total of 98 games. Career-wise, Walters won 198 and Derringer won 223 games!

Bobo the Hobo

Bobo Newsom was a unique pitcher.

First, he won 211 major league games and two World Series contests (Detroit, 1940). Included in those 211 wins were three consecutive 20-game seasons with the Browns and the Tigers (1938-40). On the other hand, he lost 222 big league games. That makes him the only pitcher with 200-or-more victories who has lost more games than he has won!

Second, he was one of only two pitchers who have led their league in losses four times. Pedro Ramos (1958-61) was the other pitcher who performed the dubious feat. But Newsom outdid Ramos in two ways. One, he lost 20 games three times; Ramos lost that many games only once. Second, he led the league in losses with the three different teams (the Browns, the Tigers, and the A's); Ramos copped that dubious distinction with only the Senators.

Third, he was the first — and only — pitcher in major league baseball to lose 20 games with three different teams.

Fourth, he played with nine major league clubs: he was either traded or sold 16 times. Big "Buck" might have been a free spirit. But he was never a free agent!

The Second-Divison Winner

Ted Lyons, who pitched his entire 21-year career for the White Sox, won 260 games despite the fact that his team finished in the first divison only five times and he missed three years to military service.

Three times Lyons won 20 games with a second-divison team. In fact, in his first 13 seasons in the majors, the White Sox failed to end up in the first division even once.

But Lyons still might have ended up with 300 victories if he had not missed three years during the Second World War. In the four years before the War, he averaged 13 victories per season. Had he maintained that rate from 1943-45, he would have reached the 300 mark.

At any rate Lyons had the least support of any pitcher who won 260-or-more games. Every pitcher who won more games than he played on at least one pennant-winner!

Opening Day No-Hit Ups and Downs

Two pitchers have thrown no-hitters on Opening Day: Bob Feller and Red Ames.

Feller, who pitched three no-hitters during his career, hurled his first one on the first day of the 1940 season. On that day the Indians defeated the White Sox, 1-0. In one of his two other no-hitters he won a 1-0 game, too: against the Yankees in 1946.

Ames, who pitched two no-hitters during his career, pitched his second hitless game on the first day of the 1909 season. On that day he no-hit the Dodgers for nine and one third innings.

But the Dodgers got seven hits off him before the game was over and beat him in 13 innings, 3-0!

Chandler's New Pitch

When baseball people talk about the best winning percentage pitchers of all time, they mention names like Whitey Ford, Juan Marichal, and Lefty Grove. But they rarely include the name of the best percentage pitcher of them all—Spud Chandler.

The Yankees' big righthander won 109 games and lost only 43 for a .717 winning percentage. That's the best mark of all time for any pitcher who has won 100-or-more games.

Early in his career Chandler was hampered by arm injuries. But in 1941 he came up with a slider; and he lost very few games over the last five years of his career. In fact, from 1941 to 1947, he won 77 games and lost only 27.

That's a winning percentage of .740!

Bob Lemon had a late start in the majors as a pitcher. He was 26 years old when he switched to the mound, and he didn't find his groove until two years later.

The Double No-Hit Loser

Jim Tobin of the Braves recorded a losing lifetime mark (105-112), but in 1944 he accomplished something few pitchers ever have: he pitched two no-hitters in one year.

His name is not listed in the record books next to Johnny Vander Meer, Allie Reynolds, Virgil Trucks, and Nolan Ryan, who have also pitched two no-hitters in one season. Why? Because one of Tobin's no-hitters was pitched in an abbreviated game. He threw a nine-inning no-hitter against the Dodgers in April. In June he hurled a five-inning no-hitter against the Phillies.

Nevertheless, Tobin ended the season, as he did most years, with a losing record — 18-19!

A Prince of a Hal

Hal Newhouser was probably the best pitcher that baseball has ever known during war time.

A 207 lifetime winner, he was at his peak from 1944-46 when he won a total of 80 games. In 1944 he won 29 games; in 1945, 25; and in 1946, 26. In each of the three years he lost nine contests.

He won 20 games for a fourth time — in 1948 when he copped 21, but he never again approached his effectiveness of 1944-46. During those peak years he had an ERA of 1.99.

In 1944 and 1945 he won the American League strikeout championship with 187 and 212, respectively. The following year, 1946, he struck out 275 batters, a personal high, but he did not win the strikeout crown. It went to Bob Feller, who struck out 348 batters to set a new major league record.

Feller's Lost Prime

Baseball fans like to speculate.

What if Joe DiMaggio played in Fenway Park and Ted Williams played in Yankee Stadium? What if Mickey Mantle had had sound knees? What if Bob Feller hadn't missed four years to the service during his prime?

Yes, what if Feller had not lost those four years? Overall, during an 18-year career, he won 266 games. In the two years before he went into the service, he averaged 26 victories per season. In the two years after he returned from the service, he averaged 24 wins per season. It is fairly safe to assume, after splitting the difference, that Feller would have averaged 25 wins per season during those four years that he missed from major league parks. That would have given him 366 lifetime victories and would have put him right in the midst of Christy Mathewson, Grover Alexander, and Warren Spahn. That's pretty good company.

Strikeout-wise, he would have been in his own league.

Walter Johnson leads the list in the strikeout column with 3,506 K's. Bob Gibson was the only other pitcher who has struck out more than 3,000 batters. Feller fanned 2,581. In the season before he left for the Second World War, he struck out 260 batters. In the season after he returned from the War, he fanned 348 batters. If Feller averaged 304 strikeouts a year, then split the difference between those two figures, for the four years that he missed, he would have added 1,216 whiffs to his present total. That would have given "Rapid Robert" a career high of 3,797 strikeouts.

Yes, what if Feller had not lost those four years?

Handicaps: Physical not Mental

Many players have had to overcome physical handicaps in order to get to the major leagues. Dummy Hoy, Mordecai Brown, Red Ruffing, Pete Gray, and Gene Bearden were just a few of them.

Hoy, who was deaf and dumb, played the outfield with finesse; and he never had a problem communicating with his fellow outfielders. Sam Crawford of the Reds and Tommy Leach of the Pirates would back off if Hoy made a throaty grunt: that meant that he would catch the ball. If he didn't make any sound, Crawford and Leach would run the ball down.

"Three Finger" Brown pitched without two fingers on his throwing hand. But it didn't impair his effectiveness. He got extra spin on the ball by rolling it off his thumb. His curve ball became so effective he won 229 regular seasons and five World Series games.

Ruffing won 273 regular season and seven World Series games, even though he did not have five toes on his pitching foot. But he still had the necessary explosion to throw hard. In 1932 he led the league with 190 strikeouts.

Gray, who played during the Second World War, won a position in the Browns' outfield even though he had only one arm. He hit just .218 in his one season in the majors. But that was 218 points higher than any other one-armed player has ever hit.

Bearden, who was severely injured during the Second World War, played with aluminum plates in his knee and head. Yet in 1948 he pitched the Indians to the pennant with 20 wins, and the World Series, with one win and one save.

Things didn't come easily to Hoy, Brown, Ruffing, Gray, and Bearden. But they never expected things to be easy. They knew the road to success was tough. But when the going got tough, the tough got going!

Bearden's One-Year Career

Gene Bearden, a Second World War hero, packed an entire career into his rookie season in 1948.

In the War he was on a cruiser that was sunk by a torpedo. He was seriously injured and eventually had aluminum plates inserted into one knee and in his head.

But those handicaps didn't have any adverse effect during the 1948 season. He won 20 games, including the playoff victory over the Red Sox, and lost only seven. In the World Series Bearden won one game, pitching a shutout, and saved the sixth and final game. The war hero had become a bona fide baseball hero.

That was the only good season that Bearden had. He never again had a winning season in six additional years in the majors. His won-lost record during that time was 25-31!

Branca's Number 13

Ralph Branca of the Dodgers was one of the unluckiest pitchers of all time.

"Hawk" was a good major league pitcher until he threw the ill-fated pitch that Bobby Thomson hit for the home run that clinched the 1951 pennant for the Giants. After that pitch Branca was never again a successful pitcher. The one-time 21-game winner (1947) never won more than four games in another major league season.

The numbers were all against Branca when he came in from the bull pen to face Thomson in the decisive game of the 1951 play-offs. When he walked to the mound, he had 13 wins. When he left the mound, he had 13 losses.

And the number on his back was 13!

Leaving a Legacy

Quite often a fading major league star offers words of wisdom to a promising rookie that can transform the talented newcomer into a bona fide big league super star.

Hank Greenberg and Joe Page are two examples.

After 12 years with the Tigers, "Hammerin' Hank" played out his final year with the Pirates. In that season he hit 25 home runs. But, more importantly, he taught a promising prospect, Ralph Kiner, how to cultivate his home run swing.

After seven years with the Yankees, "The Fireman" finished his final year with the Pirates, too, In that season he had no record. But the Pirates had made a valuable acquisition. For Page taught a young relief pitcher, Elroy Face, how to throw the fork ball.

In both cases the students learned so much from their mentors they eventually surpassed them in their special forte.

Greenberg hit 336 home runs and won four home run crowns; Kiner hit 369 home runs and won seven home run titles. Page won 57 games and saved 76 others; Face won 104 games and saved 193 others!

Al Benton Facing the Best

Babe Ruth and Mickey Mantle played 17 years apart in the American League, but there was one pitcher who faced both of them—Al Benton.

Benton, who was a rookie with the Athletics in 1934, faced Ruth when the "Bambino" was in his last year with the Yankees. In his last year, 1952, Benton faced Mantle, who was in his first full season with the Yankees!

Lindell's Knuckle Ball Career

There have been many cases of players who came to the major leagues as pitchers and later switched to regular positions. There have also been many cases of players who came up to the big leagues as everyday performers and later moved to the mound. But there have not been too many players who came up to the majors as pitchers, converted to the field, and then left the big time as hurlers.

Johnny Lindell was one.

Lindell came up to the majors as a pitcher with the Yankees in 1942. He won two games, both of them in relief, and lost one. From 1943-50 he played the outfield for the Yankees mostly, but briefly for the Cardinals. Twice he was a .300 hitter. Overall, he batted .273.

When the Cardinals released him at the end of the 1950 season, he returned to the minors and cultivated a knuckle ball. Three years later, he bounced back to the majors with the Pirates, who traded him late in the season to the Phillies.

In his final full season in the big leagues, he proved irrevocably that he was a better hitter than pitcher. At the bat he hit .303 with four home runs and 17 RBI. On the mound he posted a 5-16 record with the Pirates and a 1-1 mark with the Phillies.

The following year, he was out of baseball for good!

The Superchief Money Pitcher

Allie Reynolds, "The Superchief," was undoubtedly the best pitcher to have won 20 games in a major league season only once!

"Old Wahoo," who finished his 13-year career with a record of 182-107, got a late start in the big leagues. He didn't come up to the Indians until he was 28. To make matters worse, he played for three second division teams in his first four years with the Indians.

But he got a big break after the 1946 season. The Indians traded him to the Yankees for Joe Gordon, the stellar second baseman. He took advantage of his opportunity.

In eight years with the Bronx Bombers, he won 131 games and lost only 60, for a winning mark of 69 percent; and he became known as one of the greatest money pitchers of all time. In six of those eight years, the Yankees won the pennant. In six of those six years, they won the World Series, too.

Reynolds was superb in the World Series. In nine decisions he won seven games to equal the records of Red Ruffing and Bob Gibson. But Reynolds saved four World Series games, too, while neither Ruffing nor Gibson appeared in a World Series relief appearance.

The Yankees had so much faith in Reynolds that they pitched him in the opening games of the 1949, 1951, 1952, and 1953 games. In those contests the Yankees won three out of four times with Reynolds getting credit for two wins and one loss. (Johnny Sain won the other game for the Yankees in relief.) In 1947 and 1950 he pitched the second game of each Series, winning both times.

Reynolds pitched two ways during the regular season, too. He picked up 41 saves for the Yankees, registering 33 of them in his last four seasons (1951-54). But he won 20 games only once: during the 1952 season. In that year he was at his best, leading the league in ERA (2.06), strikeouts (160), and shutouts (6).

Rusty Staub (left) with Willie Mays, one of the best all-round players of all time.

A year earlier in 1951, he performed a feat that has been duplicated only three times: he pitched two winning no-hitters in one season. In his first hitless outing he outduelled Bob Feller, who threw three career no-hitters himself. In his second hitless outing, on the pennant-clinching day of the season, he proved that he was one of the coolest customers in clutch contests.

With two outs in the top of the ninth, Reynolds needed just one more out. But the hitter at the plate was Ted Williams, the most dangerous in the game. Reynolds bore down, however, and got Williams to pop the ball up behind the plate. But Yogi Berra, the catcher, dropped the ball. Williams was still alive. That's when Reynolds showed class. He patted Berra on the back and told his catcher not to worry, assuring him that he would get Williams on the next pitch.

On the following pitch Reynolds forced Williams to pop the ball up in the same spot. This time, Berra held on to the ball.

Though he was not a consistent 20-game winner, Reynolds proved, time and again, that he was a money pitcher when the pressure was on the line!

Two Highlights in a Negative Season

Virgil "Fireball" Trucks, who posted a 177-135 record for five American League teams, was one of four pitchers who has hurled two winning no-hitters in the same season.

In 1952 the Tigers' righthander held the Senators and Yankees hitless.

Every other pitcher who threw two winning no-hitters in the same season had a good year to go along with the two hitless games. Johnny Vander Meer of the Reds was 15-10 in 1938; Allie Reynolds of the Yankees, 20-8 in 1952; and Nolan Ryan, 21-16 in 1973. But Trucks' record reads the other way: he was 5-19. He completed only eight of 29 starts. And two of them were no-hitters.

The Tigers gave up on him. In 1953 they traded him to the Browns, who traded him to the White Sox the same year. He didn't pitch a no-hitter for either team. But he did win 20 games for the first—and only—time in his career!

Steady Eddie Lopat

Steady, ready, Eddie Lopat, who pitched for the White Sox, the Yankees, and the Orioles during a 12-year career, was known for his consistency.

Career-wise, during the regular season, he posted an overall record of 166-112; career-wise, during the World Series, he recorded a mark of 4-1.

He played in five World Series: on five consecutive world champions (1949-53).

But he was consistent at the plate, too. During the regular season he batted .211. During the World Series he hit .211!

Holloman's Only Complete Game

Bobo Holloman of the Browns didn't exactly write the book on how to pitch, but in his one year in the majors, in 1953, he did something that no other hurler has ever achieved.

The Browns' righthander posted a 3-7 record with a 5.23 ERA. He walked twice as many batters as he fanned, and he allowed approximately one hit per inning. In fact, he completed only one of his ten major league starts. But that complete game is the contest for which he is remembered.

On May 6, 1953, in his first start and only complete game of his major league career, he no-hit the Athletics!

Four Home Runs in the Sun

The one player in uniform on the respective days when Gil Hodges, Joe Adcock, Rocky Colavito, and Willie Mays hit four home runs in one game was Billy Loes.

When Hodges and Adcock hit their four-base blasts for the Dodgers and Braves in 1950 and 1954, Loes was a member of the Dodgers, who were involved in both games. In 1959, when

Colavito hit his circuit clouts for the Indians, Loes was dressed in the uniform of the opponents, the Orioles. And when Mays hit his round trippers in 1961 Loes was a teammate of "The Seh Heh Kid" with the Giants!

The Perfect Relief Pitcher

Bob Grim, who won 20 games as a rookie for the Yankees in 1954, did almost as well in relief as he did in starts.

In 20 starting appearances he completed eight games and won 12; in 17 relief appearances he won eight games and lost none.

The unusual thing about his relief spots is that he picked up eight decisions—all wins—without registering a save!

The Hall of Fame Lemon

Bob Lemon of the Indians had a late start in the majors as a pitcher, but he didn't let it slow him down.

By the time he found out he wasn't going to make the majors as a regular, he was 26 years old. But he switched to the mound and, after two years of on-the-job training, he found his groove. From 1948-56 he won 20-or-more games seven times.

Overall, he posted a record of 207-128. In addition, he won two games in the 1948 World Series.

Yes, Lemon had a slow start, but he had a quick finish: in 1976 he made the Hall of Fame!

Larsen's Unusual Shutout

Don Larsen, who once lost 21 games in a season and who career-wise lost more games than he won, pitched a World Series game on October 8, 1956, that no other moundsman has been able to duplicate: he threw a perfect game against the Dodgers.

On that day he outduelled Brooklyn's Sal Maglie, 2-0.

Larsen, who won four of six World Series decisions, pitched in a total of ten post-season games. Six times he started. But only once did he finish: the day he threw his perfect game.

Ironically, Larsen's shutout performance on that day matched his total of shutouts during the entire season—one!

Newcombe's American League Hex

Don Newcombe of the Dodgers, who had a 149-90 lifetime record, had probably the least success of all National League pitchers against the American League: he was 0-5 in World Series and all-star game play.

In 1949 he had a particularly bad year against the Junior Circuit—he lost three decisions. In the All Star Game he picked up his first loss, an 11-7 defeat in relief. Two additional losses came in the World Series. One of them, the opening game, defeat was a heartbreaking 1-0 loss to Allie Reynolds. Tommy Henrich's ninth-inning home run decided the game. In 1955 and 1956 he dropped one decision in each series.

Going into the 1956 World Series he was at the peak of his form. He won 27 and lost 7 during the regular season. Later he was to be named the Cy Young winner for 1956. But he couldn't get by the Yankees. In two starts he pitched just four and two-thirds innings. His most traumatic loss came in the seventh game. A pair of early two-run homers by Yogi Berra drove him to the showers; and the Yankees, behind Johnny Kucks' two-hitter, won 9-0.

Newcombe never recovered from that World Series. He had just one winning season—13-8 in 1959 with the Reds—in his last four years in the majors. During that period every batter looked like an American League hitter to Newcombe!

Spahn's Unique 20-Game Seasons

Warren Spahn, the fifth highest winning pitcher in history, had some things in common with his peer group — Cy Young, Walter Johnson, and Christy Mathewson — but he had some things which set him apart, too.

One similarity was that he endured. He pitched 21 years in the big leagues. (It could have been longer had his major league career not been interrupted by three years of military service.) Young and Johnson pitched more than 20 seasons in the big leagues. Mathewson hurled 17.

He was also a consistent 20-game winner. Thirteen times he won 20-or-more games in a season. Young won 20-or-more games 14 times, a major league record. Mathewson equalled Spahn's feat of winning 20-or-more games in a season 13 times. Johnson did it 12 times.

But the four pitchers had different patterns, too. Young won 30-or-more games in his career five times; Mathewson, three; and Johnson, twice. Spahn never won 30 games in a season.

In fact, Spahn never threatened to win 30 games in a season. The highest number of wins he ever recorded in one season was 23 — in 1953 and 1963 with the Braves. But he was a study in consistency. Eight times he won 21 games in a season. Six times he won 20 games in a row.

The second time he reached the figure of 23 wins for the Braves was in 1963. The unusual thing about that feat is that, at the time, he was 42-years old. No other major league pitcher — not Young, Johnson, or Mathewson—has won 23 games at that age!

Cheney's Curtain Call

What pitcher struck out the most batters in a game?

Well, if you said that Steve Carlton, Tom Seaver, and Nolan Ryan struck out 19 batters in a game, you would be right for a nine-inning game.

What pitcher struck out the most batters in an extra-inning game?

Well, if you said that Luis Tiant struck out 19 batters in a ten-inning game, you'd be getting close. But the actual answer is Tom Cheney of the Senators. He struck out 21 batters in a 16-inning game against Baltimore in 1962.

Cheney may hold the strikeout record for one game; but he doesn't rank in the same company as Carlton, Seaver, Ryan, and

Tiant. In an eight-year career he won only 19 games, an average of two and one half per season!

The Numbers Game

The twilight years of Early Wynn's and Robin Roberts's careers typify the modern players' conflict with the numbers game.

Wynn won only one game in 1963, his final season. But it was his 300th win. And he got it in relief. That's struggling — with satisfaction, though.

Robin Roberts struggled, too. In vain. Eleven years after his last 20-game season, he called it quits, 14 victories short of the coveted 300-win circle.

Why did these Hall of Famers put so much time and effort into so few victories at the tail end of their careers? They, like so many other great diamond men, played the game to the hilt until their number was up!

Carlton's Super-Season for the Basement Phillies

There have been some outstanding pitchers who have won 20-or-more games while performing for a last-place club, but none of them ever did it in quite the same style as Steve Carlton did for the Phillies in 1972.

Super Steve posted a 27-10 record, struck out 310 batters, and registered a 1.98 ERA. He won almost half of the games for the Phillies, who won only 59 and finished 37½ games behind the Pirates in the Eastern Division. The 27 wins and 310 strikeouts are highs for a pitcher on a last-place club; the 1.98 ERA is a low for a moundsman on a basement squad.

No stranger to highs and lows, Carlton has four times won 20 games in a season. Twice he has led the league in losses. For example, one year after he led the league in wins (27 in 1972), he paced the Senior Circuit in losses — with 20!

The A's Finger(s) Man

Relief pitchers Hugh Casey, Darold Knowles, and Rollie Fingers have performed "Iron Man" feats that no other bull pen specialists have ever equalled.

Casey, the Dodgers' late-inning stopper in 1947, came on in relief to finish six games against the Yankees in that year's World Series. In the process he won two games, saved one, and recorded a phenomenal 0.87 ERA in 10.1 innings of pitching.

Knowles, the middle inning specialist for the A's in 1973, didn't finish six games in the World Series against the Mets that year. But he did surpass Casey's performance in 1947: he appeared in all seven games. He ended the Series without a win-loss record, but he saved two games and registered a perfect 0.00 ERA in 6.1 innings of relief.

Fingers, the bull pen ace of the A's three consecutive world championships in 1972-74, performed in all but one game in each Series. In 1972 and 1973 he saw duty in six of the seven games; in 1974 he got the call in four of the five games. Incredibly, he performed in 16 of 19 consecutive games.

In 1972, against the Reds, he split two decisions. But he picked up two saves and posted a 1.74 ERA in 10.1 innings. The following year, against the Mets, he lost his only decision. Once again, however, he recorded two saves; and he lowered his ERA to 0.66 in 13.2 innings. In 1974, against the Dodgers, he won his lone decision and posted two saves. His ERA was 1.93 in 9.1 innings.

Fingers has recorded an all-time high six saves in three World Series. The previous record was held jointly by Johnny Murphy and Allie Reynolds of the Yankees, who registered four saves apiece!

Tom Seaver: The "K" King

Nine pitchers have struck out 300 batters in one season. But none of them is named Tom Seaver. That's an amazing fact, because Seaver struck out 200-or-more batters in a season for nine straight years — 1968-76. And none of the 300-K pitchers have done that!

In those nine seasons Seaver won five strikeout titles. But he never won more than two in succession. There have been four pitchers who have won six-or-more strikeout championships in a row: Walter Johnson, eight; Dazzy Vance, seven; Lefty Grove, seven; and Rube Waddell, six.

But none of those great pitchers struck out 200-or-more batters in each of the seasons during his streak. In fact, Grove failed to fan 200 batters in six of his seven seasons.

Dizzy Dean, another flame thrower, won four consecutive strikeout titles from 1932-35. But he didn't strike out 200 batters in any of those seasons. He never even struck out 200 batters in a single season!

Twenty Games a Must

Out of 154 seasons, counting both the National and American Leagues, there have been just three years in which a pitcher has failed to win 20 games.

In 1931 Jumbo Elliott of the Phillies, Bill Hallihan of the Cardinals, and Heine Meine of the Pirates tied for the National League high with 19 victories apiece.

In 1955 Whitey Ford of the Yankees, Bob Lemon of the Indians, and Frank Sullivan of the Red Sox tied for the American League lead with 18 wins each. Five years later, Chuck Estrada of the Orioles and Jim Perry of the Indians ended in a deadlock for the Junior Circuit's top spot with 18.

Ninety-eight per cent of the time at least one pitcher has won 20 games in a season!

ERA and the Live Ball

A good indicator as to whether the pitcher or the hitter dominated the game during a particular era is the list of ERA winners. An ERA below 2.00 suggests that the pitcher was in control. An ERA above 2.00 signifies that the hitter was in charge.

110

The ERA list indicates that there has been a definite pattern over the past 75 years.

From 1901 to 1920 the pitcher had a clear-cut advantage. Then it switched to the hitter. It remained with the batter until the War. Then it transferred back to the pitcher again. After the War the pendulum swung back to the hitters and remained with them until the 1960s. Over the last decade the advantage has see-sawed, with the pitchers enjoying a slight edge.

In the first 19 years of the American League's history, the leading ERA pitchers had numbers under 2.00. In 1920, when the live ball became a common subject of discussion, Bob Shawkey of the Yankees led the league with a 2.45 mark.

The best ERA averages in the Junior Circuit remained over 2.00 until 1943 when Spud Chandler of the Yankees spun a 1.64 mark. In 1945 and 1946, respectively, Hal Newhouser had ERAs of 1.81 and 1.94.

The lowest averages moved up over 2.00 again until the 1960s: with one exception in 1955, when Billy Pierce of the White Sox chalked up a 1.97 ERA. Since the 1960s Dean Chance (1964) of the Angels, Gary Peters (1966) of the White Sox, Luis Tiant (1968 and 1972) of the Indians and Red Sox, and Vida Blue (1971) of the A's have recorded numbers under 2.00. Their averages were 1.65, 1.98, 1.60, 1.91, and 1.82 respectively

The pattern is pretty much the same in the National League.

From 1901-20 the only pitchers who won the ERA with figures above 2.00 were Jesse Tannehill (1901) of the Pirates, 2.18; Sam Leever (1903) of the Pirates, 2.06; and Christy Mathewson (1913) of the Giants, 2.06.

In 1921 Bill Doak of the Cardinals captured the crown with an average of 2.58. From that year until 1942 only Dolf Luque (1923) of the Reds and Carl Hubbell (1933) of the Giants had ERAs under 2.00. They spun figures of 1.93 and 1.66.

During the War Mort Cooper (1942) and Howie Pollett (1943) of the Cardinals threaded figures of 1.77 and 1.75. The numbers then jumped over 2.00 until Sandy Koufax of the Dodgers posted figures of 1.88, 1.74, and 1.73 in 1963, 1964, and 1966, respectively. Since that time Phil Niekro (1967) of the Braves, Bob Gibson (1968) of the Cardinals, Tom Seaver (1971) of the Mets, and Steve Carlton (1972) of the Phillies have posted ERAs of less than 2.00. Their marks were 1.87, 1.12, 1.76, and 1.98.

The lowest winning ERA that has ever been posted in the National League was Mordecai Brown's 1.04 for the Cubs in 1906; the highest winning ERA ever registered in the Senior Circuit was Bill Walker's 3.08 for the Giants in 1929.

The lowest winning ERA ever chalked up in the American league was Dutch Leonard's 1.01 for the Red Sox in 1914; the highest winning ERA ever compiled in the Junior Circuit was Early Wynn's 3.20 for the Indians in 1950.

Consequently, Leonard's mark of 1.01 and Wynn's average of 3.20 were the lowest and the highest figures that have ever won a major league ERA championship!

Iron Mike

Mike Marshall borrowed a page out of "Iron Man" Joe McGinnity's book from 1972 to 1974, when the burly righthander led the National League in games pitched.

Four other pitchers have led their respective leagues in games pitched for three consecutive years: Ed Walsh of the White Sox (1910-12), Fred Marberry of the Senators (1924-26), Ace Adams of the Giants (1942-44), and Wilbur Wood of the White Sox (1968-70). McGinnity paced the Senior Circuit in games pitched for five consecutive years (1903-07) to set the major league mark.

McGinnity, primarily a starter, pitched 55 games, his all-time high, in 1903. In each of the three succeeding years, the number of games in which he appeared decreased: 51, 46, and 45.

Marshall, on the other hand, upped his number of games from season to season during his streak. In 1972 "Iron Mike" pitched in 65 games for Montreal. The following season, he appeared in 92 games for the Expos.

Traded to the Dodgers, after the 1973 season, he set a major league record when he pitched in 106 games for Los Angeles. In fact, he pitched in a phenomenal 63 percent of his team's games!

THE WORLD SERIES

Phillipe the First

In the first World Series in 1903, Deacon Phillipe of the Pirates set four records in a losing cause.

First, he started the most games—five. Second, he pitched the most complete games — five. Third, he figured in the most decisions—five. Fourth, he pitched the most innings—44.

The big righthander, who had a lifetime record of 186-109, also won three games — a total that 11 additional pitchers have tied. But Phillipe's 3-2 record was not good enough to pitch the Pirates to the world's title.

Bill Dinneen of the Red Sox won three out of four decisions to pace player-manager Jimmy Collins's club to the championship!

Four, the Magic Number

Five players have hit four home runs in one World Series: Lou Gehrig, Babe Ruth, Duke Snider, twice, Hank Bauer, and Gene Tenace.

But only one player has stretched out four triples, and only one player has banged four doubles in a Series.

In the 1903 World Series, between the Red Sox and the Pirates, Tommy Leach, a third baseman for Pittsburgh, ripped four triples. (The Red Sox won the Series in eight games, though.)

In the 1906 World Series, between the White Sox and the Cubs, the first inter-city baseball championship, Frank Isbell, first baseman for the Chisox, hit four doubles. The White Sox won the Series in six games.

And Isbell got all four of his doubles in the fifth game of the Series!

The Inferior League

Since the inception of the World Series in 1903, there has been only one year in which it was not played—1904.

In that year the Giants won the National League pennant, and the Red Sox won the American League pennant. But the Giants' owner, John T. Brush, and the Giants' manager, John McGraw, refused to play the Red Sox, claiming that the National League was the premiere organization and contending that the Giants could jeopardize their lofty standing by competing with a bunch of "minor leaguers." So the Red Sox, supported by an agreement which the two leagues had made in 1903, claimed the world's title by forfeit.

Public outrage against Brush, McGraw, and the Giants was so severe that New York, when it repeated as the National League champion in 1905, agreed to play the A's, the American League pennant winner. The Giants won the series in the five games; and the sports classic has been played continuously for 73 years.

McGraw and the Giants felt their one-sided victory over the A's in 1905 proved irrevocably that the National League was the superior league. But subsequent developments do not support that conclusion.

In 74 total World Series the American League has won 44, and the National League has won 30!

The Shutout Series

The World Series of 1905, which initiated a continuing sequence of 72 consecutive post-season matchups, was unique.

They call Reggie Jackson Mr. October, and many Octobers will come and go before another player can match Jackson's performance in the October of 1977.

First, all five games ended in shutouts. That outcome has never been duplicated.

Second, Christy Mathewson won three games in a five-game series. There have been many other pitchers who have won three games in a World Series without losing a game. But only Jack Coombs of the A's, in 1910, matched Mathewson's feat of winning three games in a five-game series. What puts Mathewson's feat in a class all by itself, however, is that all three wins were shutouts. In 27 innings, "Big Six" allowed only 14 hits and just one walk.

The Giants' other victory was recorded by Joe McGinnity, who pitched a 1-0 victory in the fourth game.

The A's scored only three runs in the entire Series. In game two they got two runs off McGinnity and one off reliever Red Ames to give Chief Bender the cushion he needed in a 3-0 victory.

The A's pitchers in the Series were remarkable, too. Neither Eddie Plank, Andy Coakley, nor Bender allowed more than two earned runs per contest.

But the Giants' pitching staff was incredible. In 45 innings of pitching, Mathewson, McGinnity, and Ames (who hurled only one inning) were superb. They allowed only three runs. And they were all unearned.

So the Giants' pitchers had an ERA of 0.00 in the Series!

Long-Range Effects

A comparison of the 1905-07 and the 1953 World Series shows how the emphasis has changed from the stolen base to the long ball.

In 1905 the Giants and Athletics stole a total of 13 bases; in 1906 the White Sox and Cubs, 14; and in 1907 the Cubs and Tigers, 25. There was an average of 17 thefts per Series. By way of contrast, in 1953 the Yankees and the Dodgers stole only four bases.

In the home run department there was not a single four-base blow hit in the 1905-07 World Series. But in 1953 the Yankees and the Dodgers hit a total of 17, still the all-time high!

Three Wins in Five Games

In 1910 Jack Coombs of the A's won three games in a five-game World Series to become the second pitcher who has ever performed this feat. Christy Mathewson, of course, was the other pitcher. But in no way was Coombs's performance in the same class with Mathewson's.

"Big Six" allowed very few base runners in the 1905 World Series—and no runs. "Colby Jack" granted approximately one hit per inning. In addition, he walked 14 batters. Mathewson passed only.

Coombs, though he was 3-0, didn't equal his performance of the regular season, when he won 31 and lost only nine. In addition, he pitched 13 shutouts, an American League record, and posted a 1.30 ERA. In the Series his ERA was 3.33.

But his teammates gave him great support. In the second game, for example, they pounded out 14 hits and scored nine runs. They also made three double plays during the A's 9-3 win.

Coombs needed all the help he could get. For he gave up eight hits and nine walks. But the Cubs, because of good defense on the A's part, stranded 14 runners!

Home Run Baker

Frank "Home Run" Baker, third baseman for the Athletics and the Yankees, won four consecutive home run titles from 1911-14; but he won his nickname for two home runs that he hit in consecutive games in the 1911 World Series.

A .307 lifetime hitter, the highest average for any American League third baseman, and a .363 batter in six World Series, Baker was one of four players to have won as many as four consecutive home run titles. Harry Davis of the A's won four

117

straight (1904-07); Babe Ruth, six (1926-31); and Ralph Kiner, seven (1946-52).

During Baker's four-year reign as home run king in the American League, he averaged ten round trippers per season. Career-wise, he hit a total of 94.

But he stunned the baseball world in the 1911 Series when he hit home runs in back-to-back games. In the second game his two-run homer defeated Rube Marquard and the Giants, 3-1. In the third game Christy Mathewson led 1-0 going to the ninth. But Baker homered to tie the game; and the A's won in 12 innings, 3-2.

Since that time, whenever people say "Home Run," they also say Frank Baker!

The Year 1920 Was First

The year 1920 was a season of many firsts.

First of all, Ray Chapman, the standout shortstop for the Indians, was killed during the season when an errant pitch by submarine ace Carl Mays of the Yankees struck him in the temple. Chapman was the first—and remains the only—player to be killed on a major league diamond.

Before the season started, Hal Chase, Heinie Zimmerman, and Lee Magee were privately banished from baseball because of rumored betting on the outcome of games in which they played. After the season ended, Ed Cicotte, Joe Jackson, Buck Weaver, Claude Williams, Chick Gandil, Happy Felsch, Fred McMullin, and Swede Risberg were barred from the game because of an alleged conspiracy on the part of the White Sox players to throw the 1919 World Series to the Reds.

The World Series of 1920 provided a number of firsts, too.

Stan Coveleski of the Indians became the first pitcher to win three games since Joe Wood performed the feat in 1912. Coveleski's performance in the Indians' five-games-to-two victory over the Dodgers was almost as brilliant as Mathewson's. In his three route-going victories, he allowed only 15 hits, one more than Mathewson; two runs, two more than Matty; and two

118

bases on ball, one more than "Big Six." Coincidentally, each of Coveleski's wins was a five-hitter. That's a first — and only — too!

Game five had three firsts. Elmer Smith, the Indians' outfielder, hit a grand slam in the first inning to become the first player to hit a four-run homer in World Series history; in the fourth inning Jim Bagby, who had won 31 games for the Indians during the regular season, hit a three-run homer to become the first pitcher to hit a circuit clout in post-season play; and in the fifth inning Billy Wambsganss, the Indians' second baseman, converted a line drive by Dodgers' pitcher Clarence Mitchell into the first — and only — unassisted triple play in World Series action.

Mitchell, by the way, grounded into a double play in his next appearance, so he batted into a record five putouts in two consecutive trips to the plate.

Joe Wood, the former three-game winner for the Red Sox in the 1912 World Series, provided another first. In the 1920 World Series he played the outfield for the Indians. (He had to give up pitching in 1913 when he injured his throwing hand, so he switched to the outfield and ended his career with a .283 batting average.) He was the first player to compete in one World Series as a pitcher and another one as an outfielder. The next year, of course, Babe Ruth became the second — and last — player to perform the feat.

Behind the Indians' success in 1920 was the incomparable Tris Speaker, who won his first and only pennant and World Series as a manager. Earlier in his career, he had played on world title teams in Boston in 1912 and 1915.

"The Grey Eagle" had his best overall season in 1920: he batted .388 and he drove in 107 runs. But he did not win the batting title that year. He finished *second* to George Sisler, who hit .407!

Records in Defeat

Carl Mays and Waite Hoyt, two great pitchers for the Yankees, set two marks in the 1921 World Series; yet the Bronx Bombers lost their inter-city matchup with the Giants, five games to three.

Mays, who was 27-9 during the regular season, pitched 26 innings in the World Series without giving up a walk. The prior record had been held by Christy Mathewson, who allowed one walk in 27 innings of pitching in the 1905 World Series. Yet Mays lost two of his three decisions.

Hoyt, who was 19-13 during the regular season, pitched 27 innings in the World Series without allowing an earned run. That equalled another mark that Mathewson had set in the 1905 World Series. But Mathewson won all three of his three decisions. Hoyt won only two of his three.

The Yankees' righthander allowed only two runs, both of which were unearned. He gave up one run in his fifth-game victory. He also gave up one run in the eighth-and-decisive game. It turned out to be the margin of victory. Art Nehf beat him, 1-0.

Mays and Hoyt had a combined ERA of 0.87 in the Series. Yet their combined won-lost record was only 3-3!

Johnson: Rescue in Relief

Many great pitchers, including Bob Feller, have failed to win a World Series game.

For a while it was feared that Walter Johnson, the strikeout king, would be on that list. Johnson, who played his entire career for the hapless Senators, finally got into a World Series in 1924 at the age of 37. But he lost his first two starts to the Giants, bowing to Art Nehf in the opener, 4-3, and going down to Jack Bentley in game five, 6-2.

Baseball fans feared Johnson would never get another chance. But in the ninth inning of the seventh game, with the score tied 3-3, Johnson came on in relief and pitched four scoreless innings. The Senators won the game and the series in the bottom of the twelfth when Earl McNeely's easy ground ball took a bad hop over third baseman Fred Lindstrom's head, enabling

Muddy Ruel to score the decisive run from second, so Johnson started off the Series, with a loss in a game that went 12 innings, and he finished the Series in a relief performance with a win in a game that went 12 innings!

The World Series Jinx

The World Series has proven to be a jinx to some of baseball's greats. The list includes Ty Cobb, Ted Williams, Stan Musial, and Willie Mays!

Cobb, "The Georgia Peach," hit .300 in all 23 full seasons that he played in the major leagues. Yet, in three World Series, he twice hit below .300 and his overall post-season average was .262, which was 105 points below his regular season average of .367! In addition, the all-time American League base-stealing champ swiped only four bases, an average of 1.3 per Series.

Williams, who hit .344 lifetime, batted a paltry .222 in his lone Series appearance. In that Series (1946) he hit safely only five times in seven games. And all five of his hits were singles!

Musial, who posted a career mark of .331, hit .300 in 18 of his 22 major league seasons. Yet, in four World Series, he batted .300 only once. Overall, his Series average was .256. "The Man," who hit 475 lifetime home runs, connected for only one four-base blow in 86 World Series trips to the plate!

Mays, a .302 lifetime hitter, did not reach .300 in one of his three World Series performances. In fact, he hit a lackluster .234 in 17 inter-league match-ups. What is the most amazing statistic of all, however, is that "The Seh Heh Kid," who hit 660 career homers, failed to hit one in 64 official World Series at-bats!

Surprise Starters

There have been many surprise starting pitchers in the opening game of the World Series.

Howard Ehmke, the 35-year-old A's pitcher who defeated the Cubs in 1929, was one. Jim Konstanty and Joe Black, two outstanding relief pitchers, were two others.

In 1950 Konstanty appeared in 74 games for the Phillies—all in relief. He won 16, lost 7, and saved 22. The Phillies' pitching staff had been overworked in the closing week of the season, though. So manager Eddie Sawyer chose Konstanty to start the Series. He did well. He allowed only five hits. But a double by Bobby Brown and two outfield flies sealed his fate. Vic Raschi out-duelled him, 1-0.

In 1952 manager Chuck Dressen of the Dodgers went with a relief pitcher too. For his starting pitcher he named Joe Black, who had appeared in 56 games during the regular season, 54 of them in relief. Coming out of the bull pen, he had won 14 games and saved 15.

He outduelled the always tough Allie Reynolds in the opening World Series game and downed the Yankees on six hits, 4-2. That starting game victory matched his total of starting game victories during the regular season—one!

The Forgotten Hero

Burleigh Grimes, the much-travelled pitcher, won 270 games, the fifth highest total in modern National League history; yet he was traded or sold *ten* times!

Four of his five 20-game seasons were recorded for the Dodgers. One of them was chalked up for the Pirates. But the one-time member of six different National League teams, who performed in four World Series for the Dodgers, Cardinals, and Cubs, saved his best post-season pitching outings for St. Louis.

"Ol' Stubblebeard" is the forgotten hero of the Cardinals' stunning victory over the potent Philadelphia Athletics in the 1931 World Series. Pepper Martin, the base-running hero of the Series, is generally given the credit for leading the Redbirds to their upset victory.

But Grimes, who had celebrated his 38th birthday the preceding August, won two starts—including the Series finale, 4-2—and recorded a 2.04 ERA. He ranks as the third oldest pitcher to win a World Series game.

Early Wynn was only three months shy of 40 when he picked up a starting win for the White Sox in the 1959 World Series. Wynn was one month older than Pete Alexander when Alexander gained two decisions and a save against the formidable Yankees in the 1926 World Series!

Goslin's Greatest Game

Goose Goslin, who hit .316 for three teams over an 18-year career, had some big World Series moments.

The one-time batting champ — he hit .379 for the Senators in 1928 — played every inning of every game for Washington in World Series competition. In 1924, the year that the Senators won their only world's title, he hit .344. Six of his 11 hits came in succession; a record for a series that still stands. (Thurman Munson of the Yankees tied the mark in the 1976 World Series.) In 1925 and 1933 he hit .308 and .250, respectively.

In 1934, at the age of 34, the Senators traded him to the Tigers, with whom he played in back-to-back World Series. In 1934 the Bengals lost to the Cardinals in seven games, but in 1935 they defeated the Cubs in six games.

Goslin didn't hit for high averages in either Series—.241 and .273—but he saved one of the biggest hits of his career for his last World Series appearance: in the bottom of the ninth inning, he singled home Mickey Cochrane with the run that gave the Tigers their first World Series championship!

The Substitute Catcher

Jimmy Wilson was a full-time coach for the Reds during the regular 1940 season; but he was the all-round playing star for the world's champs during the World Series.

A .284 lifetime hitter, the righthanded-hitting catcher had settled down to life as a coach after 17 National League seasons. With Ernie Lombardi handling the catching chores, there was no reason to believe Wilson would ever again don the "tools of ignorance" during another major league game.

123

In 1908 Addie Joss of the Indians pitched the second perfect game of the twentieth century.

But midway through September, Lombardi sprained his ankle and Wilson was reactivated. Down the stretch, "Ace" batted only .243, but he warmed up by Series time.

He handled the serves of two-game winners Bucky Walters and Paul Derringer faultlessly; and he swung a torrid bat, hitting .353 in the six games he played.

In addition, the 40-year-old catcher stole the only base of the Series!

Pesky's Pause (?)

One of the most dramatic plays in World Series history occurred in the bottom of the eighth inning of the seventh game of the 1946 World Series when Enos Slaughter scored from first base on a single by Harry Walker to give the Cardinals a 4-3 victory over the Red Sox.

Baseball historians have blamed Johnny Pesky, the Red Sox' shortstop, for permitting Slaughter to score. Not anticipating that Slaughter would continue to the plate, Pesky hesitated on the relay throw before he released the ball.

But Slaughter claims he never intended to take advantage of Pesky. He has said that the determining factor in his decision to score occurred in the top half of the eighth when the Red Sox scored two runs to tie the score.

Dom DiMaggio, the excellent center fielder for the Red Sox, pulled a muscle; Leon Culberson, a reserve outfielder, ran for him. With two outs and Slaughter on first base in the bottom of the eighth, Walker singled to left center field and Culberson fielded the ball. That's when Slaughter decided to go all the way. Later he said that if DiMaggio had been in center field, he would never have tried to score.

It was one of those things that so often makes the difference between victory and defeat. Pesky's pause didn't cost the Red Sox the 1946 World Series. Slaughter's daring—and alert—base running gave the Cardinals the edge. It might easily be said that Slaughter, who batted .300 lifetime, was a pretty fair "country" ballplayer!

Harry the Cat

Which of the following pitchers who won three games in a World Series without suffering a single reversal has posted the all-time low for ERA in the World Series: Babe Adams, Christy Mathewson, Jack Coombs, Stanley Coveleski, Harry Brecheen, Lew Burdette, Bob Gibson, or Mickey Lolich?

Brecheen, you might be surprised to learn, is the one. "The Cat" won three games in the 1946 World Series and posted an 0.45 ERA. He won two games in starts and one in relief. In the 1943 World Series he dropped his lone decision, and in 1944 he won his only decision. Overall, his World Series ERA was 0.83.

Surprisingly, the pitcher who holds the runner up ERA position to Brecheen is not a moundsman who won three games in one World Series. In fact, he's a player who's known more as a long-ball hitter than he is as a mound craftsman — Babe Ruth. "The Sultan of Swat" posted an 0.87 ERA. He was 3-0 in two World Series: 1-0 in 1916 and 2-0 in 1918. Included in his World Series exploits as a pitcher: a 14-inning complete game victory (the longest in history) and twenty-nine and two thirds consecutive scoreless innings, a record that stood until Whitey Ford broke it.

The amazing thing about Ruth's performance in 1918 is that he played two completely opposite positions: pitcher and outfield. But he did well in both. On the mound he turned in a 13-7 record. In 19 starts he completed 18 games. In the outfield he hit .300. And he won the home run title with a total of 11!

The Historic Farewell

In the 1947 World Series three players — Bill Bevens, Cookie Lavagetto, and Al Gionfrido — came out of relative obscurity to figure prominently in the seven-game set between the Yankees and the Dodgers. Afterwards they slipped back into obscurity. But they are still remembered today for the pivotal parts they played in the 1947 World Series, one of the most dramatic of all time!

In game four, with the Yankees holding a one-contest advantage over the Dodgers, Bevens, a pitcher with a modest 7-13 record during the regular season, made World Series history. And he also silenced critics who had questioned manager Bucky Harris's selection for the important start.

With one out remaining in the game, Bevens held tenuously to a 2-1 lead. Up to that point Bevens had neutralized the effectiveness of the Dodgers' big bats: he had not allowed a single base hit. That is not to say, however, he had not allowed a single base runner. Fighting control problems, he had granted ten bases on balls. Two of them, plus a sacrifice and an infield out, had cost him a run in the fifth inning. But it was the last two walks which Bevens yielded that cost him most dearly.

In the ninth inning he walked Carl Furillo for pass number nine. With two outs Dodger manager Burt Shotton inserted super-sub Al Gionfrido as a pinch-runner. Gionfrido promptly stole second base. The Yankees then intentionally walked Pete Reiser, who gave way to pinch-runner Eddie Miksis. That set the stage for Lavagetto, who batted for Eddie Stanky. Lavagetto responded with a double off the wall in right field to break up the no-hitter and, more importantly, win the game for the Dodgers. During the regular season Lavagetto had hit only one double.

Gionfrido, who scored the tying run in game four, prevented the tying run from scoring in game six with one of the most memorable defensive plays in World Series history.

The Yankees, who had won game five on Joe DiMaggio's home run off Rex Barney, had hopes of wrapping up the Series in game six. Once again it was DiMaggio who almost provided them with the impetus. But, with the Dodgers leading 8-5 in the sixth, Shotton once again went to his bench. And once again he called on Gionfrido, whom he inserted in left field as a defensive precaution.

Right away Gionfrido justified the move. DiMaggio boomed a 415-foot shot to the bull pen in deep left center field. But Gionfrido, who broke with the crack of the bat, made a circus catch to prevent a homer that would have tied the game. The Dodgers won the game 8-6 so the catch turned out to be both a game-saving and Series-saving theft.

The Dodgers came up with the sensational plays in the 1947 World Series; the Yankees with the most wins. Bevens got an opportunity to share in the decisive win. In the seventh game the Dodgers took a 2-0 lead when they knocked Spec Shea out of the box with two runs in the top of the second. But Bevens replaced Shea and held off the Dodgers' bats for two and two-thirds innings. He pitched scoreless ball while granting just two hits. The relief stint was important. For the Yankees pecked away at the Dodgers' pitchers with one run in the second and two runs in the fourth to take a 3-2 lead.

Ironically, Bobby Brown got the key hit in the fourth when he pinch-hit for Bevens and doubled home the tying run. Henrich's single scored Brown with what proved to be the winning run in the 5-2 contest.

Joe Page relieved Bevens and allowed just one hit in five solid innings of pitching.

Technically, Bevens was the pitcher when he left the game; and he could have recorded the win. But the official scorer gave the victory to Page, who had pitched brilliantly. In retrospect, it seems to be one additional slight to Bevens's performance in the 1947 World Series. He pitched sensationally, but not well enough to win.

Bill Bevens did not win another major league game. In fact, he never again appeared in a major league game. Nor, for that matter, did Cookie Lavagetto or Al Gionfrido. All three were dropped in 1948!

Pinch-Hitter's Delight

The 1947 World Series was a pinch-hitter's delight.

Cookie Lavagetto, of course, broke up Bill Bevens's no-hitter with a double that gave the Dodgers a 3-2 victory in game four. But the Yankees had their pinch-hitting heroes too.

128

In the third game rookie Yogi Berra, who was to eventually set so many World Series records, hit the first pinch-hit home run in World Series history.

But the "Golden Boy" tag of the Series went to another Yankees' rookie, Bobby Brown. He hit safely in three pinch-hit appearances to set a World Series record. His third successful pinch-hit was a double that scored the tying run in the final game. Tommy Henrich then singled Brown home with what proved to be the winning run of the Series.

Those three safe pinch-hits were the harbinger of an excellent World Series career for Brown. In four World Series Bobby Brown batted 1.000, .500, .333, and .357. His lifetime average in World Series play was .439!

The Substitute Runner

Who was the first black pitcher to appear in a World Series game?

Names like Satchel Paige, Don Newcombe, Joe Black, Jim "Mudcat" Grant, and Bob Gibson come to mind. Paige was the first black pitcher who threw off the mound in a World Series. He pitched two thirds of an inning for the Indians in 1948. Newcombe was the first black pitcher who was involved in a decision. He lost to Allie Reynolds and the Yankees in the opening game of the 1949 World Series, 1-0. Black was the first black pitcher to win a decision. He defeated Reynolds in the opening game of the 1952 World Series, 4-2. Grant was the first black pitcher to win two games in one Series. He did that against the Yankees in 1964. And Gibson was the first black pitcher to win three games in the same Series. He performed that feat against the Red Sox in 1967.

But none of them was the first in a World Series game. That honor belongs to a pitcher who never won a game outside of the nine he chalked up for the Dodgers in 1950—Dan Bankhead.

In game six of the 1947 World Series, manager Burt Shotton inserted him as a pinch-runner for Bobby Bragan!

Opening Game One-Run Outings

Eighteen times a World Series game has ended in a 1-0 decision. Three of those 18 times the mound duel took place in the opening game. The three times occurred in consecutive years: 1948 to 1950.

In 1948 Johnny Sain of the Braves nipped Bob Feller of the Indians; in 1949 Allie Reynolds of the Yankees outduelled Don Newcombe of the Dodgers; and in 1950 Vic Raschi of the Yankees edged Jim Konstanty of the Phillies.

The 1948 game ended in controversy. In the eighth inning the Braves put runners on first and second with one out. Feller then whirled and threw to manager Lou Boudreau in an attempt to pick Phil Masi off second base. Most of the non-partisan witnesses thought that Feller had caught Masi. But umpire Bill Stewart called the Braves' runner safe. After Sain flied out, Tommy Holmes singled Masi home with the winning run. Feller, who never won a World Series game, lost a heartbreaking two-hitter.

There was no controversy in the 1949 opener. Reynolds, who also pitched a two-hitter, came out the winner. Newcombe, who pitched a five-hitter, was the loser when Tommy Henrich homered in the bottom of the ninth.

The 1950 opener also ended with the winning pitcher allowing just two hits and the loser yielding five safeties. Raschi pitched the two-hitter. Konstanty, who had not started a game all season long in 74 mound appearances, hurled a strong five-hitter. But he was victimized when Bobby Brown, a good World Series hitter, doubled in the fourth inning and moved up two bases on outfield flies.

In 1949 Preacher Roe of the Dodgers shut out Raschi and the Yankees, 1-0, in the second game to establish a record: it was and is the only time the first two games of the World Series have ended in reverse 1-0 decisions.

The only pitcher to win two 1-0 World Series decisions was Art Nehf of the Giants. In 1921 he edged Waite Hoyt of the Yankees in the eighth-and-final game, and in 1923 he outduelled "Sad Sam" Jones of the Yankees in the third game. That year, however, he lost the final game to Herb Pennock, 6-4!

World Series Double Play Twins

If a poll were taken to determine who was the best all-round player of all time, the names of Joe DiMaggio and Willie Mays would be up at the top of the list.

But "The Yankee Clipper" and "The Seh Heh Kid" were far from their best in separate Series scenes. DiMaggio hit into a record seven double plays in 51 World Series games. Mays hit into a record three double plays in the fourth game of the 1951 World Series!

Kuzava to the Rescue

Casey Stengel had the ability to convert a journeyman starting pitcher into an effective spot relief pitcher. And his greatest success with this type of pitcher was with Bob Kuzava.

Kuzava, a lefthander who posted a 49-44 lifetime record during a ten-year career, pitched with the Yankees from 1951-54. He won 23 games and he lost 20. But he was an effective two-way pitcher for Stengel: especially in relief. In 1951, 1952, and 1953 he won five, three, and four games in relief. During those same years he saved five, three, and four games in relief.

"Sarge's" biggest two saves, however, came in World Series play. Both followed similar patterns and clinched the World Series for the Yankees.

In the sixth game of the 1951 Series, he relieved Johnny Sain in the top of the ninth, with the bases loaded and no one out, the Yankees leading, 4-1. He got Monte Irvin and Bobby Thomson on sacrifice flies. But the gap closed to 4-3. He then retired Sal Yvars on a slicing line drive to Hank Bauer, who made a sensational sitting catch; and the Yankees won their third consecutive world's title.

The following year, he relieved Vic Raschi with the ses loaded, with one out, and the Yankees leading in the top e seventh, 4-2. The first batter he had to face was Duke Snider, who had already hit four home runs in the Series. He got Snider on a pop up to the infield, though; and he also got Jackie Robinson, who followed, on an infield pop up. Billy Martin, the Yankees' second baseman, had to make a great shoestring catch on Robinson's pop up, when first baseman Joe Collins lost the ball in the sun. Kuzava then mowed down the Dodgers in the eighth and ninth; and the Yankees won their fourth straight world's title.

Kuzava hit his personal high in 1952. He won only nine games during his remaining four years in the majors. But he was the first relief pitcher — Will McEnaney of the Reds (1975-76) has been the only other one — to pick up saves in the final game of the World Series in back-to-back years!

The Big Cat's Five Paws

Johnny Mize, one of the most devastating hitters of his time (1936-53), never played in a World Series when he was in his prime; yet he played in five in the twilight of his career.

A .312 lifetime hitter, "The Big Cat" batted better than .300 in his first nine seasons in the big leagues. During that time he won every major batting laurel, including four home run titles, three slugging titles, two RBI titles, and one batting average title. But he had the misfortune to be playing with good teams at the wrong times. While he was with the Cardinals (1936-41), the Giants won two pennants; while he was with the Giants (1942-49), the Cardinals won four pennants and three world titles.

Then, late in 1949, when his batting average slipped below .300 for the second season in a row, the Giants sold him to the Yankees.

In four-plus seasons with the Yankees, "Big Jawn" never hit .300. In fact, his lifetime average with the Yankees was an ordinary .262; and his home run average with the Yankees was only 11 per season. But he became a pinch hitting specialist. In 146 substitute plate appearances for the Bronx Bombers, he hit

132

safely 41 times for a solid .284 average; in World Series pinch-hitting action he hit safely three times in eight at bats for .375.

His 1952 World Series performance against the Dodgers pointed out his value to the Yankees. He hit safely six times in 15 at bats for a .400 average. Three of his six hits were home runs, one of them coming in a pinch-hitting role. During the regular season the 39-year-old lefty had hit only four home runs. In the World Series he hit three—on successive days!

Mize, though no longer the potent slugger he had once been, bowed out of the majors in super style: he played his last five years on world championship teams. No other player has ever retired so gracefully.

Martin: Series Superstar

Many average players during the regular season play like super-stars in the World Series. Billy Martin of the Yankees is a good example.

A .257 lifetime hitter, with a career high of .267 in 1952, he slugged the ball at a .333 clip during five World Series, with a post-season high of .500 in 1953. In his last three (1953, 1955-56), he batted .500, .320, and .296.

During regular season play he hit 64 home runs in 3,419 at bats, an average of one home run every 53 times he came to the plate. In World Series play he ripped five home runs in 99 at bats, a rate of one home run every 20.

A clutch player, he was at his best in 1952 and 1953. In the second game of the 1952 World Series against the Dodgers he hit a three-run homer that broke open a 2-1 game. The Yankees went on to win, 7-1. He started and ended the 1953 World Series, also against the Dodgers, in grand fashion. In the first inning of the first game he tripled with the bases loaded to catapult the Yankees to a 9-5 victory. In his final at bat, in the sixth and deciding game, he singled home Hank Bauer with the game-winning and championship-clinching run. Overall, he got 12 hits in 24 at bats for a .500 batting average. That performance tied him with Davis Robertson of the Giants (1917) for the

133

highest average in a six-game Series. His 12 hits put him in a class by himself. No other player has ever recorded 12 hits in a six-game Series.

In addition to batting .500 in the 1953 World Series he hit two home runs, two triples, and two doubles to compile an incredible .958 slugging average!

But another aspect of his World Series play has gone virtually unrecognized — his defense. He did not make an error over a stretch of 23 consecutive games, a World Series record for a second baseman!

The most important play he made came in the seventh inning of the final game of the 1952 Series. It should have been a routine play, but it almost won the Series for the Dodgers. With the bases loaded and two out, Jackie Robinson lifted a high fly ball near the pitcher's mound. Joe Collins, the first baseman, lost the ball in the sun; Bob Kuzava, the pitcher, froze on the mound. Two runners had already crossed the plate and the third one was rounding third when Billy Martin alertly bolted from second base and made a shoestring catch to prevent the Dodgers from scoring three runs on an infield pop-up and winning the seventh-and-deciding game.

Instead, the Yankees held on and won, 4-2!

Rhodes: A Risky Pinch-Hitter

Career-wise, Dusty Rhodes was less than a mediocre pinch-hitter; but for one season, 1954, he was probably the best clutch-hitting pinch-hitter in the history of baseball.

In 1954, the year the Giants won the pennant and swept the Indians in the World Series, Rhodes seemed to come through every time he stepped to the plate with men on base in a pinch-hitting situation. Actually he made 15 hits in 45 late-game appearances for an average of .333. Overall, he batted .341 and belted 15 home runs.

In the World Series that year he made four hits in six plate appearances. Pinch-hitting, he hit safely all three times he stepped to the plate. All three pinch-hits were timely. In the first

Joe Morgan won the Most Valuable Player Award for the Cincinnati Reds both in 1975 and 1976.

135

game he hit a three-run homer in the bottom of the tenth to provide the winning margin in the 5-2 game. The following day his pinch-hit single tied the game at 1-1. He then went into left field and iced the game that the Giants won, 3-1, with a long homer in the seventh inning. In the third game he delivered a pinch-hit single with the bases loaded to score the runs that turned out to be the tying and the winning counters.

But his star faded. Four years later he was out of the big leagues. His seven-year pinch-hitting average was an anemic .212.

The Versatile Infielder

Gil McDougald was one of the most versatile players ever to perform in World Series play.

The Yankees' infielder, who played in eight World Series during his ten years in the majors, played three different positions in post-season games: third base, shortstop, and second base.

He has been the only infielder who played three different positions on world championship teams: from 1951-53 he played third base, in 1956 he played shortstop, and in 1958 he played second base.

The Little Slugger

Bobby Richardson, a .266 spray-hitting lifetime batter, turned slugger in the 1960 World Series against the Pirates.

In 30 at-bats he got 11 hits, including two doubles, two triples, and a grand slam home run for a .367 average. In addition, he drove home 12 runs for the Yankees in the seven-game Series to set a record that still stands. He capped his performance off with a .667 slugging average.

During the regular season he batted .252, hit *one* home run, drove home 26 runs, and slugged the ball for a .298 average.

World Series time brought out the best in Richardson. In 1964 he closed out his World Series career the way he began it—with a bang. He got 13 hits—a Series record—in 32 at-bats for a .406 average. The only other player who got 13 hits in World Series play was Lou Brock, who hit that total for the Cardinals in a losing cause to the Tigers in 1968.

When Richardson set his RBI record in 1960, and his total hit record in 1964, the Yankees lost the World Series, too!

The Ghost of Greatness

By the end of the 1962 season, it was apparent to the Yankees that it was time for the old pro, Bill Skowron, to give way to the young rookie, Joe Pepitone. So the Yankees traded Skowron to the Dodgers to open the first base job for Pepitone. But by the end of the 1963 World Series, it was also apparent that the old pro still had a few tricks he could teach the young rookie.

The 1963 regular season didn't start out or end up that way, though. Pepitone moved into the starting line-up and hit a solid .271 with a respectable total of 27 home runs. On the other hand, Skowron displayed signs of being over the hill. He hit only .203 and tagged just four home runs.

But when the World Series money was on the line, it was a different story. Skowron hit .385 with one home run and three runs batted in. He singled home two clutch runs in game one and homered in game two to give Johnny Podres a late-game cushion in his 4-1 win.

Pepitone, in the meantime, got just two hits in 13 at-bats for an anemic .154 average. He failed to drive one run home; and he lost a throw by third baseman Clete Boyer in the white shirts of the spectators in the third-base boxes, to allow the winning run to score in game four.

In fact, the Dodgers swept the once-powerful Yankees in four straight games!

Six-Time Losers

Pee Wee Reese of the Dodgers was one of the best shortstops the Dodgers ever had, and Elston Howard was one of the best

137

catchers the Yankees ever had. But they also have a more dubious distinction: each of them played a record six times on a losing World Series team.

Reese played on five straight losers with Brooklyn (1941, '47, '49, '52-'53) before he played on a winner in 1955. Those five straight losers tied him with Fred Merkle, who never played on a winner. But Reese set the major league record of playing on six losers, in 1956, when the Dodgers lost to the Yankees in seven games.

Howard had more team success in World Series play than Reese: he played on four winners (1956, '58, '61-'62). But he also played on six losers (1955, '57, '60, '63-'64, and '67).

They each share the major league record for most Series on a losing team, and they each hold their respective league record for most Series on a losing team. They also hold separate league records: Reese holds the league record for most Series on the *same* losing team; Howard holds the league record for most Series on *separate* losing teams. Reese played his entire career with the Dodgers. Howard played most of his career with the Yankees. But he also played with the losing Red Sox in the 1967 Series.

The Strikeout Record Makers

There have been many outstanding strikeout performances by starting pitchers in World Series games.

In 1906 Ed Walsh of the White Sox raised eyebrows when he struck out 12 Cubs in one game. That record stood until Howard Ehmke of the Athletics fanned 13 Cubs in 1929. Twenty-four years later, in 1953, Carl Erskine raised the whiff record to 14 in a superb performance against the Yankees. That mark stood until Sandy Koufax set down 15 Yankees in the first game of the 1963 World Series. Finally, in 1968, Bob Gibson elevated the record to its present level when he struck out 17 Red Sox batters.

But only one pitcher has struck out double figures in a relief performance—Moe Drabowski. In the opening game of the 1966

World Series, the Orioles' righthander struck out 11 Dodgers in six and two thirds innings!

McLain and Lolich

Going into the 1968 World Series, Denny McLain was the ace of the Tigers' pitching staff, and Mickey Lolich was the Bengals' number-two man. But, coming out of the Series, the roles were reversed: Lolich was the ace of the staff and would remain so for the rest of his stay with the Tigers.

In 1968, during the regular season, McLain won 31 games and lost only 6. His ERA was an impressive 1.96. But in the World Series he won only one of three decisions and posted a 3.33 ERA.

Lolich ended up 17-9 during the regular season. His ERA was a mediocre 3.19. But in the World Series he was 3-0 with a respectable 1.67 ERA.

After McLain won 24 games the following year, he faded into obscurity. He wound up his career with the Braves in 1972. Lolich, on the other hand, went on to become a two-time 20-game winner.

Both of them left their mark: McLain was the last pitcher to have won 30 games in a season; and Lolich has whiffed more batters than any other lefthanded pitcher in the history of baseball—2,799!

An Old Story

The Los Angeles Dodgers and the New York Yankees hit a combined total of 17 home runs in the 1977 World Series, tying a record that the two teams had established and later tied.

In 1977 the Dodgers hit nine round-trippers — Reggie Smith banged three of them—and the Yankees clouted eight four-base blows — Reggie Jackson smashed five of them.

That tied the record for the most home runs in a six-game series. In 1953 the Yankees poled nine home runs and the (Brooklyn) Dodgers, eight. Two years later, the Yankees again cracked nine circuit clouts and the Dodgers, eight. But that was in a seven-game series.

The Dodgers also tied the 1953 Yankees for the most team home runs in a six-game series — nine. The Yankees of 1956 hit 12 homers, the most four-base blows that any team has ever hit in a seven-game World Series!

The Money's on Munson

Thurman Munson, who won the American League's MVP Award in 1976, is regarded in big-league circles as a money player.

A .291 lifetime hitter, he has batted .300 and driven home 100 runs in each of the past three seasons. The last player before Munson to achieve that feat was Bill White (1962-64) of the Cardinals.

In the 1976 World Series Munson batted a blistering .529; in the 1977 World Series he tailed off to a very respectable .320. The last six times at bat in the 1976 World Series, he hit safely to tie the record that Goose Goslin of the Senators established in the 1924 World Series. The first time up in the 1977 World Series, he singled to run his consecutive hits in World Series play to seven — the all-time high.

Perhaps what is even more extraordinary is that Munson has played in ten World Series games and has batted safely in each one of them!

Mr. October

They call Reggie Jackson Mr. October. And with good reason.

In the 1973 World Series Jackson hit .310 and one home run with the A's. One year later, he stroked .286 and one homer for Oakland. In 1977, with the Yankees, he smashed .450 and five home runs.

After a slow start in the 1977 World Series, Jackson ended up with one of the best series that any player has ever had.

He hit the ball for 25 total bases, breaking the former record of 24 which was set by Duke Snider and tied by Lou Brock. Both Snider and Brock needed seven games to record their totals, though. The previous six-game record was set by Billy Martin, Jackson's manager, who amassed 23 total bases.

Jackson also scored ten runs, one better than the former record held by Babe Ruth.

Some other records which Jackson set: four consecutive home runs (with one walk in between), four home runs on four consecutive swings, three straight homers in one game, three homers on three swings in one game, three home runs on the first pitch in one game, and three homers off three different pitchers in one game.

In fact, Jackson hit three home runs off three different pitches in the sixth game of the 1977 World Series. Burt Hooten threw him a slider, Elias Sosa served him a sinking fastball, and Charlie Hough offered him a knuckleball.

But Jackson's most impressive feat was hitting five home runs in one Series. No player had ever done that before. Not Babe Ruth, Lou Gehrig, Duke Snider, Hank Bauer, or Gene Tenace, all of whom hit four homers in one series. (Snider performed the feat twice.)

Many Octobers will come and go before any other player has the kind of sensational series that Reggie Jackson had in the October of 1977!

Not only was Ty Cobb the greatest hitter of all time, he was probably the greatest batting coach too.

THE MANAGERS

Lajoie: No Napper

Nap Lajoie, who was elected to the Hall of Fame in 1937, was so esteemed by the Cleveland fans for his skill at second base and with the bat that the owners named the club after him.

While the .339 lifetime hitter was the manager of Cleveland, from 1905-09, the club was nicknamed the "Naps!"

The Stahl Saga

In one six-year period the Stahl brothers, Chick and Jake, managed the Red Sox with tragic and successful consequences.

Chick, the older, was popular with Red Sox fans. He was popular with members of the opposite sex, too. In 1902 a Fort Wayne stenographer, who claimed that Stahl had jilted her, tried to shoot him. She was unsuccessful. But Stahl, a .305 lifetime hitter, must have been unnerved: he never hit .300 again during his major league career.

In the waning days of the 1906 season, he replaced the once successful Jimmy Collins as manager. When he took the club over, it was in last place; when he finished the season, it was still in last place.

Stahl's 5-13 record as manager of the Red Sox preyed on his nerves during the off-season. He finally suffered a nervous breakdown. So in 1907 he relinquished his managerial duties.

But he went to spring training as the club's captain. Before the season started, however, he unexplainedly swallowed a bottle of carbolic acid and died in the arms of Collins, his friend, his roommate, and his former manager.

One year later, his wife, Julia, to whom he had been married for only five months, died mysteriously in South Boston.

Jake, the younger brother, had begun his career as a first baseman with the Red Sox in 1903. He then drifted to Washington and New York. In 1908, one year after his brother's death, he returned to the Red Sox. Two years later, he won the league's home run crown with ten round trippers.

In 1912, after a one-year layoff, he was offered the Red Sox manager's position. He accepted it and made the most of his only full year as a major league skipper: he led the Red Sox to their first pennant since 1904 and their second World Series triumph!

Double Play Managers

Joe Tinker, Johnny Evers, and Frank Chance, immortalized in a poem by sportswriter Frank Adams, are the most famous double play combination in baseball history.

But they were good, too. They led the Cubs to four pennants and two world titles in the first decade of this century.

At one time or another, they were all managers. Chance guided the Cubs during their glory days of the early 1900s. The playing manager hit .296 lifetime.

Evers, who batted .270 lifetime, led the Cubs in three spaced-out seasons without notable success; and Tinker, who hit .262 lifetime, directed the Reds, the Chicago entry in the Federal League, and the Cubs. He led the Federal League franchise to a first-place finish in 1915.

Tinker, Evers, and Chance, who excited the Windy City with their footwork around first and second base, all managed the Cubs. They have been the only famous double play combination in history who also managed the team for which they starred!

McGraw: The Superstitious Strategist

Baseball players are superstitious. But not many have gone to such extremes as John McGraw in the years 1911-13!

Before a game in St. Louis, early in the 1911 season, a tall, lanky individual approached manager McGraw and told McGraw he had just come from a fortune teller who told him that if he would join the New York team and pitch for it, the Giants would win the pennant.

McGraw was skeptical but curious. The Giants had not won a pennant since 1905. McGraw, it has been said, would do anything to win. So he gave the pitcher, who identified himself as Charles "Victory" Faust, a chance to show his stuff. Pretty soon McGraw was catching Faust barehanded.

But, intrigued by the fortune-teller's prophecy, McGraw let Faust hit and run, too. He soon found out that Faust couldn't do any of those things, either. That night, however, when the Giants' train left for Chicago, Faust was on it.

Every remaining day in the 1911 season, Faust warmed up before the game, thinking that he was going to pitch. But he rarely did. In fact, he pitched only two innings all year. In two relief appearances he gave up one run and two hits in two innings for a 4.50 ERA. But the Giants won the pennant!

So Faust returned to the Giants the following year. And the McGrawmen won the pennant again, although Faust did not appear in one single game!

In 1913 McGraw had his lucky charm dressed in a Giant's uniform every day, waiting for his manager's urgent call. By this time Faust had become a celebrity. His reputation had spread around the league. Wherever the Giants went, the fans clamored for Faust to make an appearance. One day in Cincinnati the Reds stayed on the field for a fourth out, just so Faust could make an appearance. The Reds let him hit the ball and then slid him into second, third, and home while the fans howled in delight.

Charles "Victory" Faust had become so popular that a theatrical firm signed him to a contract for $400 a week to do six shows a day. He would dress in uniform and humorously imitate Ty Cobb, Christy Mathewson, and Honus Wagner. The audiences loved it.

But, as soon as Faust left the team, the Giants lost four games in a row. That was too much for Faust, who left the stage and returned to his beloved Giants. He said simply that the Giants needed him more than Broadway did. The Giants immediately got back on the victory track and went on to win their third consecutive pennant.

That winter Faust fell ill and died. In 1914, the following baseball season, the Giants did not win the pennant.

The Midas Touch

Ed Barrow, who never played in the major leagues, had the Midas touch when it came to getting the most out of ballplayers.

In the late 1890s he discovered Honus Wagner, who later won eight batting championships for the Pirates. In 1903 and 1904 he managed the Tigers to second-division finishes. And he put together the machinery that eventually won three straight pennants from 1907-09. In 1918 he took over the managerial duties of the Red Sox and led them to a pennant and world title. But, more importantly, in the same year he switched Babe Ruth from being primarily a pitcher to an everyday player. Ruth justified the move by winning the first of his 12 home run championships.

Barrow managed the Red Sox for two more years, when he saw a pattern beginning to take shape. Owner Harry Frazee, who was in financial difficulty, was selling talent by the ton to the Yankees. So Barrow moved to New York, too, when owner Jake Ruppert offered him the general manager's job in New York. In 1921, his first year in New York, the Yankees won their first pennant.

"Cousin Ed" was the GM in New York for 25 years. During that time the Yankees won 14 pennants and ten world championships!

The Peerless (?) Leader

Frank Chance, "The Peerless Leader," was another one of those managers who had initial success as a field leader; but he faded from the big league scene with his clubs on the bottom end of the eight-team standings.

Named the manager of the Cubs midway through the 1905 season, he brought the Bruins home third. In the next three years (1906-08) he led the Chicago nine to three pennants and two World Series victories. After a second-place finish in 1909, he brought Cubs home first once again. But the A's defeated them in the World Series, four games to one.

Chance, a .296 lifetime batter, saw his average slip from .298 in 1910 to .241 in 1911 to .200 in 1912. The Cubs slipped with his batting average. They finished second in 1911 and third in 1912.

Washed up as a player, he found himself out of a manager's job in Chicago. He moved to New York, where he directed the Highlanders to two seventh-place spots in the standings. (Actually Roger Peckinpaugh replaced him for the final 12 games of the 1914 season and lifted the Highlanders' finish in the standings to sixth.)

After eight years out of baseball, Chance made a one-year managerial comeback with the Red Sox in 1923. But an eighth-place finish prompted him to hang up his spikes for good. In his first three full seasons as a manager in the big leagues, his teams won three straight pennants; in his last three "full" seasons as a manager in the majors, his teams finished either one game out of the basement or in it.

Lefty O'Doul, a .349 lifetime hitter, often said that a manager, no matter who he was, couldn't win unless he had the "horses." As proof, he would point to Chance's success with the Cubs and his failure with the Red Sox.

Frank Chance with the Red Sox, he would say, didn't have a "chance."

The Comforts of Retirement

Many managers have come out of retirement. Some have ended up happy, some sad. Bill Carrigan of the Red Sox was one who rued the day he left the comforts of retirement.

In 1913 he first got his chance to manage when he replaced Jake Stahl 81 games into the season. When he took over the Red Sox, they were in fifth place; when he finished the season, they were in fourth. After a second-place finish in 1914, he led the Bosox to pennants and world championships in 1915 and 1916. Then he retired . . . for the first and glorious time.

Eleven years later he returned to the managerial wars with the same Boston franchise. But not with the same results. The Red Sox ended last in all three of the years that he guided their destiny.

Then he retired . . . for the last and ignominious time!

The Tigers' Talented Tutor

Just about every baseball fan knows that Ty Cobb was the greatest hitter of all time. Not too many are aware, however, that he was most probably the greatest batting coach who ever lived, too.

In 1921, when he became the manager of Detroit, he lifted the team's batting average from .270 in 1920 to .316—an increase of 46 points. Only the 1930 New York Giants have compiled a higher team average—.319! During his six-year tenure as skipper of the Tigers, he proved his team's 1921 statistics were no accident. From 1921-26 the Bengals averaged .302.

Cobb's greatest protégé was Harry Heilmann, who won four batting titles and recorded a lifetime average of .342. Before Cobb became the manager of the Tigers, Heilmann's career mark for his first six years in the major leagues was .282. After Cobb assumed the reins in Detroit, Heilmann did an about-face. He averaged .380 for the following seven seasons, winning batting titles in four alternate years: 1921, '23, '25, and '27. In

1923 he became one of only eight players ever to hit .400. That year he hit the ball at a .403 clip.

But his greatest thrill came in 1921 when he won the batting title with an average of .394. In second place, five points behind at .389, was his manager and batting tutor, Ty Cobb!

The A's Playing Managers

Three Hall of Famers who became playing managers ended up on the Athletics as players in 1928: Ty Cobb, Tris Speaker, and Eddie Collins.

Cobb, after 22 years with the Tigers, including six as a playing manager, moved to the Athletics in 1927 and wound up his playing career in 1928. In his final season the .367-lifetime-hitter batted .323. In all 23 of the full seasons that he played in the majors, he batted better than .300.

Speaker, after 20 years with the Red Sox, Indians, and Senators, including eight years as the playing manager of the Tribe, ended his career with the A's in 1928, too. A .344 lifetime hitter, he batted .267 in 1928—only the second time in the last 20 years of his career that he had failed to hit .300.

Collins, who started his career with the A's and was traded to the White Sox, finished his baseball playing days where he started them—in Philadelphia. A .333 career batter, he returned to the A's in 1927, the same year that Cobb joined Connie Mack, after serving as the playing manager for the White Sox in 1925 and 1926.

In 1926 all three of the Hall of Famers were playing managers for teams other than the A's. In 1928 they ended their careers with the A's. Collins actually played until 1930 as a player-coach, but he batted only nine times his last two years in the big leagues.

In 1928, while three Hall of Famers were in the twilight of their careers with the A's, four other eventual Hall of Famers were just beginning to build bright futures for themselves: Jimmy Foxx, Al Simmons, Lefty Grove, and Mickey Cochrane.

There were a total of seven Hall of Famers on the 1928 A's. And yet they finished second, two and one half games behind the Yankees!

The Old Timers

Connie Mack, who managed until he was 88 years old, had an affinity to old-time ballplayers.

He demonstrated that vividly in the 1929 World Series, which the Athletics took from the Cubs, four games to one. In game one he pitched 35-year-old Howard Ehmke, who, during the regular season, had started only eight games, completed just two and thrown only 55 innings!

But Ehmke rewarded his skipper's faith in him with a 3-1 win. En route to his surprise victory, Ehmke struck out 13 Cubs to establish a World Series record! It stood until Carl Erskine of the Dodgers whiffed 14 Yankees in the 1953 World Series.

In game four, with the A's leading in the Series, two contests to one, he again went with experience. This time he chose Jack Quinn, who won 242 games, as his starter. What was surprising about the selection was that Quinn was 45 years old. The oldest starter in World Series history gave up five runs in five innings. But the awesome A's staged a ten-run rally in the seventh inning to score a come-from-behind 10-8 victory.

But Mack did not lose confidence in Quinn. The following year, he pitched Quinn in a two-inning relief stint against the Cardinals. So Quinn was not only the oldest pitcher ever to have started a Series game, he was also the oldest pitcher—46—who has ever relieved in a Series game.

The 1929 World Series was unusual. One of the most unusual occurrences of the Series happened in the second game. George Earnshaw and Lefty Grove combined to stop the Cubs, 9-3. The amazing part of their performance, however, was the fact that they struck out 13 batters between them. In 26 years of World Series history, no pitcher, before 1929, had ever struck out 13 batters in a game. And then, in back-to-back games three of the A's pitchers jointly hurled 13 strikeout games in succession!

Cobb and Carl

If Ty Cobb, the manager, could have developed pitchers the way he hit them, he might have been a Hall of Fame skipper, too. But Cobb, who had so much success in teaching his hitters how to make safe contact against opposing pitchers, had difficulty teaching his pitchers how to stifle enemy bats.

During his six-year tenure as manager of the Tigers, he had only one 20-game winner, Hooks Dauss, who turned in a 21-13 record in 1923. In fact, Dauss was the only Bengal pitcher who won 20 games during the period of 1919-33. He won 21 games in 1919, too. In 1934 Tommy Bridges and Schoolboy Rowe ended the famine when they turned in records of 22-11 and 24-8.

The Tigers, under the direction of playing manager Mickey Cochrane, won back-to-back pennants in 1934-35 with Bridges and Rowe serving as the leaders of the pitching staff. Alvin Crowder and Eldon Auker were respectable back-up moundsmen; but if Cobb had shown a little more foresight in the 1920s, the Tigers would have had the most formidable staff in baseball during the 1930s.

But Cobb didn't. He released a future Hall of Famer. A pitcher who would win 253 games in the National League. A moundsman who would pitch in three World Series and win four of six games. A hurler who would fan five mighty American League sluggers — in a row — in the 1934 All Star Game. A craftsman who was in the midst of five consecutive 20-win seasons when the Tigers were winning pennants in 1934-35.

That's right, Ty Cobb, the greatest hitter of all time, cut Carl Hubbell, one of the greatest pitchers of all time!

Minor League Dynasties

Occasionally, in the history of baseball, there have been great teams in the minor leagues who could beat most of the clubs in the major leagues. The Baltimore Orioles of the 1920s and the Newark Bears of the 1930s are two examples.

Both teams played in the International League.

The Orioles won seven straight International League pennants from 1919-25. With the players that they had on their roster, it's no wonder that they did. In 1920 the Orioles had former major league players Fritz Maisel, Jack Bentley, and Ben Egan. They also had future major leaguers Lefty Grove, George Earnshaw, Al Thomas, Joe Boley, Max Bishop, Rube Parnham, and Johnny Ogden.

Grove, who went on to win 300 major league games, stayed with the Orioles for five years. In those days there was no big league draft and the Orioles, who were owned and managed by generous Jack Dunn, paid their players more than most major league clubs did. Grove made $750 a month and $1,800 every year the Orioles won the Little World Series, which pitted the winner of the International League and the winner of the American Association against each other. Finally, Dunn sold Grove to Connie Mack and the Athletics for $100,000.

The investment paid off. From 1929-31 Grove pitched the A's to three pennants and two world titles. Earnshaw, Boley, and Bishop were also vital cogs on those championship teams.

The Bears of the 1930s were another incomparable minor league team. In 1937, for example, they won the International League pennant by 25½ games. In the Little World Series they lost the first three games at home, but they rebounded by winning four straight at Columbus to win the Triple-A championship.

From that team, the starting infield, the starting outfield, the two catchers, and the entire pitching staff graduated to the majors. (Phil Page, one of the pitchers, had been in the majors before he joined the Bears.) The infield comprised George McQuinn at first, Joe Gordon at second, Nolan Richardson at short, and Babe Dahlgren at third. Charlie Keller, Bob Seeds, and Jimmy Gleason made up the outfield. The catchers were Buddy Rosar and Willard Hershberger; the pitchers were Spud Chandler, Atley Donald, Steve Sundra, Vito Tamulis, Joe Beggs, and Marius Russo.

In the following two years Gordon, Dahlgren, Keller, Chandler, Russo, Sundra, and Donald moved up to the parent Yankees and helped the Bronx Bombers complete their four consecutive world championships (1936-39). After they got edged by the Tigers and Indians in 1940, they bounced back to win three pennants and two world titles.

Like the Orioles of the 1920s, the Bears of the 1930s formed one of the greatest dynasties in the history of the minor leagues. The key personnel of both teams eventually moved up to the Athletics and Yankees to form two of the greatest dynasties of the major leagues!

Managers in Their Twenties

Casey Stengel was a septuagenarian when he managed the Yankees to their last pennant in 1960, but many skippers have been in their twenties when they got their first chance to direct a major league club.

Roger Peckinpaugh, Lou Boudreau, and Joe Cronin are three examples.

Peckinpaugh was the youngest manager ever to finish a season, Boudreau was the youngest signal caller ever to start a season, and Cronin was the youngest field leader ever to win a pennant.

At the age of 23, Peckinpaugh was named the fill-in manager of the Highlanders for the last 17 games of the 1914 season. He didn't get another chance to guide a major league club until he began a six-year stint with the Indians in 1928.

In 1941 he returned to the Tribe for a second aborted tenure at the helm. The following year, he was replaced, ironically, by Boudreau, who was only 24 years old. Six years later, Boudreau led the Indians to their first pennant and World Series victory in 28 years.

Cronin guided the Senators to a pennant in 1933, his rookie year, at the age of 26. One year later, he brought the Nats home seventh. The following year, he was sold to the Red Sox for $250,000. What was unusual about the sale of Cronin is that Clark Griffith, the man who cashed in on him, was his father-in-law!

The Grimm Chance

Outside of Frank Chance, Charlie Grimm has been the most successful manager of the Cubs. Chance won four pennants and Two World Series in eight years. Grimm won three pennants in 14 years.

Grimm made a smash debut in 1932. With 57 games remaining in the season, he became the manager of the second-place Cubs; and he brought the club that formerly belonged to Hornsby to the National League pennant.

In 1938 he suffered the same fate as Hornsby. With 73 games remaining in the season and the Cubs contending in third place, Gabby Hartnett replaced Grimm and brought the Bruins home first.

On two other occasions, in 1935 and 1945, when owner Phil Wrigley permitted Grimm to handle the reins from the beginning of the season to the end of the year, the deft first baseman rewarded his boss with two pennants.

Chance and Grimm had a couple of other things in common. In his eight years with the Cubs, "The Peerless Leader" never finished worse than third; in his first seven years with the Bruins, "Jolly Cholly" never finished worse than third, either. And in their final years of managing, Chance with the Red Sox in 1923 and Grimm with the Cubs in 1960, both of them ended up last.

But Grimm has been the only manager to take over a contender midway through a season and bring the club home first, and the only skipper to relinquish the reins of a contender midway through a season to a successor who brought the team home first!

Leo Durocher stunned the baseball world when, halfway through the 1948 season, he switched from the Dodgers to the Giants.

A Champion Skipper in Two Leagues

Three managers have won pennants with teams in both leagues: Joe McCarthy, Yogi Berra, and Alvin Dark.

McCarthy guided the Cubs to a pennant in 1929 and the Yankees to league flags in 1932, '36-'39, and '41-'43. Berra led the Yankees to a first-place finish in 1964 and the Mets to a loop crown in 1973. Dark paced the Giants to a league title in 1962 and the A's to a circuit championship in 1974.

There have been many managers who have won pennants with two teams in the same league, but there has been only one to win pennants with three clubs in the same league: Bill McKechnie, who guided the Pirates (1925), Cardinals (1928), and Reds (1939-40) to first-place finishes!

A Game of Inches

Baseball, they say, is a game of inches. Managing is a position of games. An inch this way, or an inch that way, and a game may be won or lost. A game this way, or a game that way, and a manager's position may be either won or lost.

Bucky Harris, who got good mileage out of his 5-foot-9-inch 155-pound baseball body, came within a couple of games of perhaps reaching baseball immortality.

At the age of 28 the steady second baseman was named the playing manager of the Senators. Harris justified owner Clark Griffith's faith in him with back-to-back pennants in his first two years (1924-25) as the Nats' skipper. The .274-lifetime-hitting pivotman was the only Senators' manager to win two pennants. In 1924 he added Washington's lone World Series victory to his managerial laurels.

In 1929 he moved his dual-role position to Detroit, where he assumed the second of his eight managerial positions—a major league record. He managed Washington on three different occasions; Detroit on two. Overall, in 29 years he called the shots for five different teams. He ranks third to Connie Mack (53) and John McGraw (33) in years of managerial service.

Twenty-three years after he led Washington to its first pennant, he guided the New York Yankees to a pennant and World Series victory. Only Connie Mack had a longer gap (1902-31) between his first and his last pennant.

Harris was also one of the three pennant-winning playing managers who also won a league flag as a bench leader. The other two were Joe Cronin (Senators in 1933 and Red Sox in 1946) and Leo Durocher (Dodgers in 1941 and Giants in both 1951 and 1954).

The itinerant baseball skipper might have gained himself a permanent niche in Cooperstown, however, if he had "managed" to win the 1948 pennant with the Yankees.

Unfortunately, he finished third, three games behind the Indians and two games behind the Red Sox. If he had won, he would have been rehired in 1949; and he—not Casey Stengel— might have led the Yankees to consecutive world championships from 1949-53.

Seven consecutive world championships. Now that would be something to talk about. Especially at the Hall of Fame in Cooperstown!

The Tribe's Playing Managers

The Indians, who have won three pennants and two world titles, have had more success under playing managers than they have had under dugout skippers.

In 1920 the Tribe won the pennant and world championship under playing-manager Tris Speaker, "The Grey Eagle," who had the best year of his career, batting .388 and driving home 107 runs.

In 1948 the Tribe won its first pennant and world crown in 28 years, this time under the inspirational leadership of playing-manager Lou Boudreau, who batted .355 and drove home 106 runs. In the season's play-off game against the Red Sox, Boudreau homered twice to lead the Indians into the World Series.

Six years later (1954), the Indians won their third—and last— pennant under bench manager Al Lopez, who guided the Tribe to 111 victories, an American League record.

But the Indians failed to win a game in the World Series. The Giants swept them in four straight.

The Patient Managers

"They also serve who only stand and wait."

Burt Shotton and Fred Haney must have been familiar with that line for they had to wait until they got the chance to manage a good club.

Before Shotton took over the Dodgers in 1947, he had managed the Phillies from 1928-33. His best finish during those six years was fourth, and his average finish was sixth. But when Leo Durocher was suspended from baseball for one year in 1947 for associating with gamblers, Shotton got his chance to guide the Dodgers, and he made the most of it. He led Brooklyn to its first pennant since 1941.

The following year, Durocher was reinstated and resumed his position at the reins of the Dodgers. But, midway through the season, with the Dodgers struggling in fifth place, general manager Branch Rickey rehired Shotton; and Durocher took over the Giants. The Dodgers finished in second place.

In 1949 the Dodgers won the pennant again under Shotton's direction. They did well in 1950, too. In the closing week of the season, they closed a big gap that the Phillies had had. The race went down to the final day. In fact, it went into extra innings. But Dick Sisler's three-run homer gave Robin Roberts and the Phillies the game and the pennant.

After the 1950 season Shotton retired. But his record in Brooklyn was impressive: two pennants and two second-place finishes in four years.

Haney's career was similar to Shotton's. From 1939-41 he managed the Browns, who finished eighth, sixth, and seventh during those years.

In 1953 he got a second chance with the Pirates. But he was dismissed after he led the Bucs to three eighth-place windups.

He got his third — and biggest — break in 1956 when he replaced Charlie Grimm as the manager of the Braves midway through the season. Milwaukee was in fifth place when he took command of the Braves, but he got them together and they finished the season second. In the next two years he guided the Braves to back-to-back pennants, including a world title in 1957.

The following year, the Braves finished second after losing to the Dodgers in a playoff series. Haney retired after the 1959 season. But he left behind him the most successful managerial record in the history of the Braves' franchise: two pennants, one world title, and two second-place finishes in four years.

Haney's and Shotton's patience paid off. When Haney won his first pennant he was 59 years old. When Shotton won his first he was 62 years old. No manager older than Shotton has ever won a first pennant!

Lopez: The Second-Place Champ

Al Lopez, manager of the Indians and the White Sox, may not have had the best record for first-place finishes in managerial history, but he has had the best mark for second-place endings.

In 16 years of managing, his teams finished second ten times. During that time they also won pennants in 1954 (the Indians) and 1959 (the White Sox).

In his first nine years of managing (1951-59), his teams finished no worse than second. They won two pennants and finished second seven times, each time to the Yankees!

Unusual Trades

The trade of Chuck Tanner, the former manager of the A's, for Manny Sanguillen, the former catcher of the Pirates, seems unorthodox; but there have been other unusual deals during the past two decades.

Two of them involve the Indians and the Tigers.

Slightly more than half way through the 1960 season, the Indians and Tigers agreed to swap Joe Gordon and Jimmy Dykes. What was unconventional was that there were no players involved in the deal. The Indians and Tigers traded managers, even-up.

Gordon had once been involved in a deal in which both teams benefited. Before the 1947 season the Yankees traded Gordon, their second baseman, to the Indians for Allie Reynolds, the pitcher.

"Flash" Gordon gave the Indians a short-term return whereas "Superchief" Reynolds gave the Yankees a long-term dividend. In 1948 Gordon hit 32 home runs and drove home 124 runs while the Indians won their first pennant and World Series in 28 years. From 1947-54 the Yankees won six pennants and World Series while Reynolds posted a 131-60 record.

But neither the Indians nor the Tigers gained from the Gordon-Dykes trade. The Indians were in fourth place when Gordon moved to Detroit, and they were in fourth place at the end of the season. The Tigers were in sixth place when Dykes switched to Cleveland, and they were in sixth place at the end of the season. One year later, Gordon was the manager of the Kansas City Athletics, and Dykes wound up his 21-year managerial career.

In the off-season, before the Gordon-Dykes swap, the Indians and the Tigers shocked the baseball world with a straight player deal: Rocky Colavito for Harvey Kuenn. The strange part about that trade was that in 1959 Colavito led the league in home runs, with Cleveland, while Kuenn led the league in batting, with Detroit!

The Last Will Be First

Strange as it may seem, the longer it takes a manager to win a pennant, the more successful he generally turns out to be!

Fourteen managers have won pennants in their first season. Nine of the 14 went on to win consecutive pennants, but all nine failed to win thereafter. Hughie Jennings (1907-09), Mickey Cochrane (1934-35), and Ralph Houk (1961-63) are three examples. After their initial victories they managed for 25 combined seasons without winning a pennant.

160

Sparky Anderson could turn out to be an exception to the first-year jinx. Anderson led the Reds to pennants in 1970, his frosh season, and in 1972; he guided them to pennants and world titles in 1975 and 1976.

Eleven skippers have won league championships in their second season. Frank Chance of the Cubs won four pennants and two world titles in his first six years as a field leader. He failed to win another pennant in five years as a manager. In fact, in 1923, his last year as a pilot, he brought the Red Sox home last.

Walter Alston has been a key exception to the sophomore jinx. He won pennants in 1955-56, 1959, 1963, 1965, 1966, and 1974.

Nine skippers have won league honors in their third year; and eight—including Joe McCarthy (nine pennants and seven world titles) and Billy Southworth (four pennants and two world titles)—have copped league laurels in their fourth season. Fred Clarke (two pennants and one world title), Connie Mack (nine pennants and five world titles), and Bill McKechnie (four pennants and two world titles) have won in their fifth year. Three managers, including John McGraw (ten pennants and three world titles), won their first pennant in their sixth season.

George Stallings, Lou Boudreau, Mayo Smith, and Gil Hodges won in their seventh year. Each won only one pennant, but they did so in an interesting fashion. Stallings piloted "The Miracle Braves" in 1914; Boudreau, the last playing manager to win a pennant, guided the Indians to their first pennant (1948) in 28 years; Smith directed the Tigers in 1968 to their first pennant in 23 years; and Hodges controlled the destiny of "The Amazin' Mets" in 1969.

Burt Shotton (two pennants) and Fred Haney (two pennants and one world title) won in their eighth year, and Miller Huggins (six pennants and three world titles) won in his ninth season.

But Casey Stengel, no stranger to irony, is the most amazing. The most successful manager over a 12-year period — he won ten pennants and seven world titles — he did not win his first flag until his tenth year, the longest it took any pennant-winning manager to win a league crown!

Early Wynn performed in the major leagues during four different decades. He retired in 1963, when he won only one game—his 300th.

162

THE TEAMS

The National or American (?)

There have been many arguments down through the years as to which League is stronger: the National or American. The truth is that there have been times when the Junior Circuit reigned supreme, other times when the Senior Circuit reigned supreme.

But to Jim Bunning, who seemed to have had an equal amount of success in each league, neither organization was too tough to tackle.

Bunning spent the first nine years of his 15-year career with the Tigers in the American League. During that time he won 108 games and lost 87. He also struck out 1,406 batters and pitched a no-hitter. On July 20, 1958, he set down the Red Sox without a safety.

In 1964 he was traded to the Phillies in the National League. His six-year statistics with the Phillies, Pirates, and Dodgers read almost the same as with the Tigers. He won 116 games and lost 97. He also struck out 1,449 batters and pitched a no-hitter.

If one had to say whether Bunning was better in one league rather than another, one might lean toward the National League. In the Senior Circuit he won a few more games and struck out a few more batters. He also pitched a *better* no-hitter.

On June 21, 1964, he pitched a perfect game against the Mets. It was the first victorious perfect game in National League history!

The A's Hot Corner

At one time or another the Athletics had three of the best third basemen in American League history on their roster: Home Run Baker, Joe Dugan, and George Kell. But they let all three of the hot cornermen go.

Baker, who batted .307 during a 13-year career, won four home run titles and played in four World Series with the A's. But they sold him to the Yankees, and he played in two additional World Series in New York.

Dugan, who batted .280 over a 14-year career, played with the A's during his first five years in the majors. But, once again, the A's sold him to the Yankees; and he played in five World Series in New York.

Kell, who batted .306 for 15 years, played the first four years of his career with the A's. But he was traded to the Tigers with whom he won the American League batting title with an average of .343 in 1949.

Baker's and Kell's lifetime averages are numbers one and two, respectively, for third basemen in American League history!

The National League Tamers

What team enjoyed the most successful decade of baseball in major league history?

The Yankees is correct. The Yankees of the 1930s won five pennants and five world championships, four of them in succession (1936-39). Joe McCarthy was the Yankees' manager during their most successful decade. The Yankees of the 1950s, under the direction of Casey Stengel, won eight pennants (the most won by any team during a decade) and six world championships, the most won by any club during a decade. But their world title percentage was *just* 75. The Yankees of the 1930s had a 100 percent world title mark.

What team enjoyed the most successful decade of baseball, under multiple managers, in major league history?

The Yankees, again? No. The best the Yankees did in one decade under multiple managers was during the 1940s when they won five pennants and four world titles under McCarthy, who won three pennants and two world titles; Bucky Harris, who copped one pennant and one world crown; and Casey Stengel, who took one pennant and one world championship.

But they didn't have a spotless world title record during the 1940s. They did lose *once*; in 1942, to the Cardinals.

There have been two teams in the history of the game who have won three-or-more world titles in one decade, under multiple managers, without losing any.

The Oakland A's, of recent memory, won three straight world titles under Dick Williams (1972-73) and Al Dark (1974). But there has been one other team that was even more successful during one decade than the A's: the 1911-19 Red Sox, who won world championships in 1912 (Jake Stahl), 1915-16 (Bill Carrigan), and 1918 (Ed Barrow).

During the same era the Giants suffered the worst fate of any team that played in the World Series a multiple number of times in one decade. John McGraw, the most successful manager in National League history, guided his Giants to four pennants; but he directed them to four World Series defeats, too!

The Giants' Lack of Lady Luck

For a team that won seven pennants between 1912 and 1924, the Giants had unbelievably bad luck during that stretch. They won only two of the seven World Series. If Lady Luck had smiled on the Giants, they would have won five of the seven World Series.

In 1912 the Giants lost to the Red Sox in eight games. (One of them ended in a 6-6 tie.) However, they held a one-run lead going to the bottom of the ninth in the final game. But center fielder Fred Snodgrass dropped a fly ball and first baseman Fred Merkle and catcher Chief Meyers allowed a pop foul to drop. Tris Speaker then singled home the tying run, and Larry Gardner hit a sacrifice fly to score the winning run.

In 1917 the Giants lost to the White Sox in six games. Once again the winning run scored in tragic fashion for the Giants. Heinie Zimmerman, the Giants' third baseman, made a two-base throwing error; Dave Robertson, the right fielder, muffed a fly ball; and Zimmerman ended up chasing Eddie Collins across the plate with the winning run when home was left unattended.

In 1924 the Giants lost to the Senators in seven games. They should have won the game and the Series in regulation time, 3-1. But a ball that took a bad hop over Fred Lindstrom's head at third enabled two runs to score. The tied game was won in the twelfth inning. Hank Gowdy, the Giants' catcher, got his foot caught in his mask on a pop foul, giving Muddy Ruel a second chance. Ruel then doubled. He scored when Earl McNeely's ground ball hit a pebble and bounced over Lindstrom's head.

Manager John McGraw, who refused to play the Red Sox in the 1904 World Series, must have had a premonition. Or maybe the Giants' ill fate was just an example of poetic justice designed to humble the proud McGraw. At any rate, McGraw's World Series record was three wins and six losses. But it just as easily could have been six wins and three losses!

Boston Sells Out

Between 1911 and 1919 the Red Sox were undoubtedly the most successful baseball team. Conceivably they could have become the most successful franchise in the history of baseball. But they sold tomorrow for today.

Owner Harry Frazee needed cash. Colonel Jake Ruppert, the owner of the Yankees, was the man who could provide it. And Frazee had a valuable commodity that Ruppert wanted — talented ballplayers. In order to get the money which he so desperately needed, Frazee had to part with the nucleus of the Red Sox team. Between 1919 and 1923 he sold Babe Ruth, Carl Mays, Wally Schang, Waite Hoyt, Everett Scott, Joe Bush, Sam Jones, and Herb Pennock to the Yankees.

166

Ruth, Schang, and Scott moved immediately into the regular lineup for the Yankees at right field, catcher, and shortstop. Mays, Bush, Jones, Pennock, and Hoyt became the nucleus of pitching rotations that established the Yankees' 1920s dynasty.

In 1918 Mays, Bush, Ruth, and Jones won a total of 65 games for Boston. In 1922, 1923, and 1924, former Red Sox pitchers won 70, 76, and 65 games for the Yankees. Overall, Mays, Bush, Jones, Ruth (who pitched in only five games for the Yankees), Hoyt, and Pennock won a total of 1,203 major league games. That's an average of 201 games per pitcher!

Ruth, of course, rewrote the record book. In addition to turning in a .671 percentage as a pitcher (94-46), he batted .342, clubbed 714 regular season home runs, and belted 15 four-base World Series blows.

The Yankees, stocked with former Red Sox talent, went on to win 21 world titles. (They had never won even one before.) The Red Sox, since they unloaded their superstars to the Yankees, have not won another since!

One would think that the Red Sox had learned an expensive lesson. But, in 1930, when the A's had replaced the Yankees as the perennial American League pennant winners, the Red Sox sent Red Ruffing, a two-time 20-game loser to New York.

With the Yankees Ruffing won 20 games four years in succession (1936-39) and went on to have a great career: he won a total of 273 regular major league games, and he turned in a 7-2 record in World Series play.

But, most importantly, he got the Yankees back on the winning track, pacing them to seven pennants and six world championships!

The Phillies' Façade

The 1930 Phillies compiled a .315 team batting average. That's a record—for a team that finished in last place!

Even today's players would be impressed with the averages of the regulars on the 1930 Phillies: first baseman Don Hurst (.304), second baseman Fresco Thompson (.304), shortstop Tommy Thevenow (.286), third baseman Pinkey Whitney (.342), left fielder Lefty O'Doul (.383), center fielder Denny Sothern (.280), right fielder Chuck Klein (.386), and catcher Spud Davis (.313).

They weren't one-time wonders, either. Careerwise, they hit an impressive .299 average.

With any kind of a pitching staff, the Phillies could have made a run for the pennant. But the 1930 Phillies didn't have any kind of a pitching staff. Most pitchers throw baseballs to the plate. The Phillies' pitchers threw time fuses. They exploded on contact.

In 1930 the Phillies' batters accounted for 6.1 runs per game. But the Phillies' pitchers allowed 7.7 runs per contest. Their closest rival, the Pirates' hurlers, finished a distant second in that department with 6.0 runs granted per game.

The Phillies' pitchers were the most consistent leaders on their team. But they led the league in negative categories: ERA (6.71), hits per game (13.07), and bases on balls per contest (3.56).

In 1930 the Cardinals had a team batting average of .314, one point lower than the Phillies. Both teams could hurt their opponents with the bat. But there was one slight difference between the two teams: the Cardinals finished first; the Phillies, last!

Baseball's Best Outfields

The best hitting outfields of all time were the Tigers (1921-29), the Athletics (1924-32), and the Pirates (1925-33).

The Tigers were the best of the three. During their nine-year hitting spree, they had eight flyhawks hit better than .300 in a season: Ty Cobb, Harry Heilmann, Bobby Veach, Heinie Manush, Al Wingo, Bob Fothergill, Harry Rice, and Roy Johnson.

From 1921-29 only twice did a Detroit outfielder fail to hit .300 in a season. Both times the player was Manush, who ended up his career with a .330 lifetime average. In 1924 he hit .289; in 1927, .297.

During that period the Tigers' outfielders had a combined average of .350.

The Athletics were the second best of the three. During their nine-year hitting splurge, they had seven ballhawks hit better than .300 in a season: Bing Miller, Al Simmons, Bill Lamar, Walt French, Ty Cobb, Mule Haas, and Doc Cramer.

From 1924-32 only three times did a Philadelphia outfielder fail to hit .300 in a season. In 1926 Lamar hit .284, in 1930 Haas batted .299, and in 1931 Miller hit .281.

During that time the Athletics' outfielders had a combined average of .332.

The Pirates were the third best of the three. During their nine-year batting binge, they had eight green pasture men hit better than .300 in a season: Kiki Cuyler, Max Carey, Clyde Barnhart, Paul Waner, Lloyd Waner, Fred Brickell, Adam Comorsky, and Fred Lindstrom.

During that era only four times did a Pittsburgh outfielder fail to hit .300 in a season. In 1926 Carey hit .231, in 1931 Comorsky batted .243, in 1932 Comorsky hit .286, and in 1933 Lloyd Waner batted .276.

From 1925-33 the Pirates' outfielders had a combined average of .325.

Over those nine-year periods the Tigers, the Athletics, and the Pirates fielded what amounts to 27 sets of flyhawks and 81 total ballhawks. Never during that time did a trio of outfielders fail to average .300 in a season.

Overall, the Tigers', the Athletics', and the Pirates' outfielders compiled a .336 batting average over a 27-year period.

No Shut-Outs

The Yankees once went 308 games (Aug. 2, 1931-Aug. 3, 1933), the equivalent of two 154-game schedules, without being shut out. No other team has ever gone through an entire season without being blanked.

The Way It Was

American League teams don't make RBI hitters the way they used to. Well, maybe American League teams don't make RBI hitters the way the Yankees used to make them.

It's a rare season when the Junior Circuit produces five hitters with 100 RBI-or-more. In fact, in 1971, Harmon Killebrew of the Twins was the only batter in the loop who reached the 100 RBI level: he led the league with 119.

But the 1937 Yankees had five hitters who topped the 100 RBI plateau: Lou Gehrig, 152; Joe DiMaggio, 125; Tony Lazzeri, 109; George Selkirk, 107; and Bill Dickey, 107. That's a record, of course. The five Yankees combined to drive home 600 runs, an average of 120 per player.

The last time an American League batter drove home 120 runs was in 1970 when Frank Howard of the Senators finished the season with 126 RBI!

Power without Average

The Yankees have won 25 home run titles (Babe Ruth and Lou Gehrig tied for the League lead in 1931), but they have copped only six batting crowns.

Babe Ruth, Lou Gehrig, Joe DiMaggio, George Stirnweiss, and Mickey Mantle have been the Yankees' batting titlists. Only one of them won it twice—Joe DiMaggio.

"The Yankee Clipper" won back-to-back titles in 1939 and 1940!

The Tigers' Attack

Excluding the pitcher, the Tigers could field an entire team of .300 hitters if they had all played their careers at the same time!

Consider this infield: Hank Greenberg, .313; Charley Gehringer, .320; Harvy Kuenn, .303; George Kell, .306; and Mickey Cochrane, .324. How about this outfield: Ty Cobb, .367; Harry Heilmann, .342; and Sam Crawford, .309?

If you needed a substitute outfielder or pinch-hitter, you could call upon David Dale Alexander, .331; Heinie Manush, .330; Goose Goslin .316; and Bobby Veach, .310.

Eight Tigers, including Al Kaline, have won 22 batting titles. (They have won 23 crowns if one counts David Dale Alexander, who won the title in 1932 when he played for both Detroit and Boston.) But Kaline, who hit 399 home runs, more than any other Bengal, couldn't break into this lineup. He doesn't have the credentials: he batted only .297 lifetime!

100 RBI Infield

Gene Bearden (20), Bob Lemon (20), and Bob Feller (19) won a total of 59 games for Cleveland in 1948; but it was the Indians' infield that was primarily responsible for leading the Tribe to its first pennant since 1920.

Eddie Robinson (83), Joe Gordon (124), Lou Boudreau (106), and Ken Keltner (119) drove in a total of 432 runs, an average of 108 RBI per player.

The preceding year, when Cleveland finished fourth, the infielders accounted for 288 runs, an average of 72 runs per man; the following year, when the Indians ended up third, they (with Mickey Vernon succeeding Robinson at first) knocked in 257 runs, an average of 64 ribbies per batsman!

Durocher . . . Robinson

Mention the names of Leo Durocher, Eddie Stanky, Sal Maglie, and Jackie Robinson in a bar on Washington Heights or Flatbush Avenue, and you're sure to start a verbal war: even though it's been twenty years since they figured in one of the bitterest rivalries in all of sports history between the Brooklyn Dodgers and the New York Giants!

Durocher stunned the baseball world midway through the 1948 season when he switched from the Dodgers to the Giants. He had managed Brooklyn for eight and one half years. He would manage the Giants for seven and one half years. The

Dodgers' fans, who once loved him, called him Judas; the Giants' fans, who once despised him, soon regarded him as their savior. That was after he led their dearly beloved Giants to a pennant in 1951 and a pennant and world title in 1954.

The Dodgers' and Giants' fans had mixed emotions about Stanky, too. When he was "The Brat" with Brooklyn, the Giants' fans booed him unmercifully. In fact, when he came to the Giants with Alvin Dark from the Braves, they still vented their long-standing spleen. But in time he, like Durocher, changed the catcalls to cheers.

In 1950 Durocher removed him from the final game when his batting average was a flat .300, and the fans gave him a standing ovation while he ran to the clubhouse in center field. Stanky, who became the playing manager of the Cardinals in 1952, finished his career with the Giants in 1951. When Bobby Thomson hit the "Home Run Heard Round The World," Stanky left the host dugout and ran to the third base coach's box, where he jubilantly jumped into the arms of Durocher, whom he alternately hated and loved. The Dodgers' fans never quite forgave him for that.

In the World Series of that year, he gave the other team in New York, the Yankees, reason to boo him unmercifully when he cleverly kicked the ball out of veteran Phil Rizzuto's glove on a tag play, to give the Giants added momentum in one of their two victories.

Maglie, because of the war and his suspension from baseball for jumping to the Mexican League, got a late start in the majors. He was 33 when he pitched his first full season with the Giants. But he made the most of the precious time he had left. He won 119 games, pitching the Giants into the World Series in 1951 and 1954 and the Dodgers in 1956. It seemed as though one out of every two wins came against the Dodgers in clutch games.

"The Barber" would walk, unshaven, out to the mound in hostile Ebbetts Field unabashedly and repeatedly knock down Carl Furillo, Jackie Robinson, Roy Campanella, and Gil Hodges while the denizens of the ballpark booed lustily. But he would invariably win in a ballpark in which Warren Spahn seldom pitched.

In 1956 Maglie was going nowhere with the Indians (0-0) while the Dodgers were waging a tough pennant duel with the Braves. This time the Dodgers called on an ex-Giant: they bought Maglie, who promptly rewarded them. He pitched them to the pennant, winning 13 of 18 decisions, including his first — and only — no-hitter against the Phillies in late September. In the World Series he split two decisions with the Yankees. The game that he lost 2-0 was the one when Don Larsen pitched the only perfect game in World Series history!

Some of the Dodgers did not forget the knockdowns, though. Jackie Robinson, when asked one day what he thought of Maglie as a pitcher, said that his one-time nemesis was a "helluva pitcher." When the same reporter probed further, wondering what Robinson thought of Maglie as a person, the second baseman replied that his teammate was a "helluva pitcher."

After the 1956 season it was apparent that Robinson's once quick legs had deserted him. So the Dodgers tried to capitalize on whatever market value he had left by selling him to — who else — the Giants!

But Robinson refused to join the Giants. Instead, he retired. He was, first and always, a Dodger!

First and Last

The 1960 Yankees outhit the Pirates, .338 to .256, they hit ten homers to the Pirates' four, and they outscored the Bucs, 55 to 27; but Pittsburgh won the World Series in seven games!

The Yankees dominated the Pirates in other hitting departments, too: safeties (91-60) and RBI (54-26). The Bronx Bombers edged the Bucs in doubles (13-11), but they distanced them in triples (4-0).

Four of the Yankees hit .400-or-better: Elston Howard (.462), Johnny Blanchard (.455), Hector Lopez (.429), and Mickey Mantle (.400). Twelve New Yorkers batted .300-or-above. Only three

Yankees who saw considerable action hit less than .300: Gil McDougald (.278), Roger Maris (.267), and Clete Boyer (.250).

It would seem as though the Pirates might have had a considerable edge in the mound statistics. Not so. The Bucs' overall ERA was 7.11; the Yankees; 3.54.

Baseball, it has been said, is a game that comes down to pitching, hitting, and fielding. The difference between the Pirates and the Yankees in the 1960 World Series was that Ralph Terry threw the pivotal pitch, Bill Mazeroski hit the historic homer, and a Buc fan fielded the fly: out in the street!

No. 42: Maris, Mantle, and Team

The 1961 Yankees, paced by Roger Maris and Mickey Mantle, hit 240 team home runs, the all-time high; but they were not the best slugging team of all time.

The 1927 Yankees, led by Babe Ruth and Lou Gehrig, hit 158 home runs, 82 less than the 1961 Yankees; but they were the best slugging team of all time.

The 1927 Yankees slugged the ball at an average of .489; the 1961 Yankees belted the ball at an average of .442.

The "Murderer's Row" Yankees of 1927 had only three players in double figures under the home run column: Ruth, 60; Gehrig, 47; and Tony Lazzeri, 18. The "M and M Boys" of 1961 had more home run balance: Maris, 61; Mantle, 54; Bill Skowron, 28; Yogi Berra, 22; Elston Howard, 21; and Johnny Blanchard, 21.

But the 1927 Yankees dominated their league more decisively than the 1961 Yankees. The former Bronx Bombers hit almost three times as many home runs as the team with the second highest number of homers — the A's, 56. Ruth alone hit more home runs than any team other than the Yankees in 1927. Only the A's, Red Sox, and Tigers hit more round-trippers than Lou Gehrig.

The 1961 Yankees hit twice as many homers as the Red Sox, A's, and Senators. But the rest of the American League teams were not distanced quite so decisively. For example, Los Angeles hit 189 team home runs; Detroit hit 180.

The difference between the team batting averages of the respective clubs accounts for the disparity between the slugging figures. The Yankees of 1927 batted .307; the Yankees of 1961 .263.

The truly amazing part of the comparison, however, is that one finds that the Yankees of 1961, who hit more home runs than any other club in one season, did not finish second, third, fourth, or fifth in the slugging race to the Yankees of 1927. They finished 42nd!

Casey's Meal Ticket

Whitey Ford, one of the most dependable pitchers of all time, was Casey Stengel's meal ticket. But ultimately Stengel lost his stub to success when he lost his appetite for his favorite dish.

In 16 years of pitching, 11 of which were spent under the watchful eye of Stengel, Ford won 236 games and lost 106 for a winning percentage of .690, the all-time high for hurlers with 200-or-more wins. During his career he pitched in 11 World Series, seven of them under Stengel. He won ten games, the all-time high, and lost eight, the all-time high in World Series play. In addition, he set a World Series mark when he pitched 33²/₃ consecutive innings of shutout ball.

His ERA during the regular season was 2.75. His ERA during the World Series was 2.71. That's consistency!

But Stengel lost his meal ticket when he deviated from what had become a consistent pattern: pitching Ford in the opening game of the World Series. After Allie Reynolds and Vic Raschi faded in 1954, Ford became the bellwether of the staff. The acknowledged Yankees' ace, he pitched the opening game of four consecutive World Series, 1955-58, another record. He won two of three decisions with Ryne Duren picking up the other victory in relief.

But, in 1960, Stengel lost faith in Ford. He did not start him against the Pirates in the opening game. In fact, he did not pitch him until the third game. That was Casey's downfall. He started Art Ditmar in the opener and came back with him in game five. Ditmar lost both games, failing to complete a total of two innings in the two games.

In the meantime, Ford was at his all-time best, pitching two shutouts in two starts. But when it became time for the seventh and deciding game, there was no Ford in the Yankees' lineup. He had pitched the third and sixth games. Had he pitched the opener, he would have pitched the fourth game and subsequently the seventh game, too. In that seventh game the Yankees scored nine runs. But their pitchers gave up ten runs!

Would Ford, who had held the Pirates scoreless for 18 innings, be able to hold the Bucs to eight runs or less in the final nine innings? The Yankees' owners, Dan Topping and Del Webb, thought so. After the 1960 World Series they fired Stengel and replaced him with his first-base coach, Ralph Houk, who led the Yankees to three straight pennants. Yogi Berra, who succeeded Houk, added another pennant to the string in 1964.

But those teams (1961-64) were basically Casey's clubs. Had he had the foresight to go with Ford, his meal ticket, in the opening game of the 1960 World Series, it's probable that he would have stayed around to enjoy his club's success in the four years that followed!

Houk: A Shadowy Figure

Ralph Houk, who led the Yankees to three pennants and two world championships in his first three years of managing, did not have a distinguished career as a player. In eight years as a reserve catcher for the Yankees, he batted a respectable .272. But he never stole a base during that time. Nor did he hit a home run.

Of course he played in the shadow of Yogi Berra, the Hall of Fame catcher. A decade later, Berra managed in the shadow of Houk, though. In 1964, after he had led the Yankees to their

Relief pitcher Rollie Fingers has recorded seven saves in three World Series, an all-time high.

third pennant in a row, Houk became the general manager of the Pinstripers. Berra, his first-base coach, was named to succeed him as the manager.

The Yankees won their fourth consecutive pennant in 1964. But Houk, along with owners Dan Topping and Del Webb, decided that Berra was too easy on his players. So, after the Yankees lost the World Series to the Cardinals, they fired him and replaced him with Johnny Keane, his counterpart in the 1964 World Series.

But Keane, who had inherited a group of fading superstars, finished sixth in 1965 and was released twenty games into the 1966 season. He was succeeded by Houk, who moved out of the shadows.

Top to Bottom and Back Again

Many baseball teams have found out it's a short way from the top to the bottom. Some teams have found out it's an equally short way from the bottom to the top.

The Giants of the 1910s proved that it takes only a short time to go in both directions. They won consecutive pennants from 1911 to 1913. Then in 1914 they finished the runner-up to the "Miracle Braves." The following year they slid to eighth place. But then they regained their stride. In 1916 they moved up to fourth, and in 1917 they won the pennant. Four years later, they reeled off four consecutive pennants.

The Athletics of the 1910s dropped more suddenly. In 1913 and 1914 the A's won back-to-back pennants. But they got swept by the Braves in the 1914 World Series. They finished in the cellar seven times in a row after 1914.

The Senators of the 1930s experienced success and failure in rapid succession. In 1933 they won the pennant. In the next year they dropped to seventh. They never rebounded.

The Dodgers' swan dive of the 1960s was just as sudden and just as severe as the A's of 1915. In 1965 and 1966 the Dodgers won pennants. But they, too, got swept by the Orioles in the 1966 Series. The following year, they dove to last place.

In the other league the Yankees' dynasty was crumbling in the 1960s, too. After they got swept by the Dodgers in 1963 and edged by the Cardinals in 1964, they dropped to sixth in 1965 and tenth in 1966.

About the same time the Red Sox were making their move — in the other direction. After ninth-place finishes in 1965 and 1966, they won the pennant in 1967.

Of course, there were reasons for the sudden about-faces.

In 1914, when the Giants slipped to second, Mathewson was finishing his string of 12 consecutive 20-game seasons. In 1915 and 1916 Mathewson's record dropped to 8-14 and 4-4. The Giants' win-loss record fell with Mathewson's win-loss mark.

Also in 1914, Connie Mack, the owner and manager of the A's, got upset with his club for its four-game defeat by the Braves. So he either sold or traded most of the stars on the team. The result was that the A's collapsed completely.

Joe Cronin was called "The Boy Wonder" when he led the Senators to the pennant in 1933. The following year he aged quite a bit. Part of the reason was Goose Goslin's departure for Detroit. The other part was the collapse of his pitching staff. In 1933 Earl Whitehill and General Crowder won 46 games. The following year they won only 18.

The Dodgers of 1967 proved that the Dodgers of 1966 had been a one-man show. In 1966 Sandy Koufax won 27 games. He retired after that season. It seemed as though the rest of the Dodgers retired with him.

The Yankees' superstars lost their once invincible skills in 1965. Bobby Richardson, Tony Kubek, Mickey Mantle, Roger Maris, Ellie Howard, and Whitey Ford turned the corner of their careers in the same season.

The rise of the Red Sox was a case of maturation. Reggie Smith added some punch to the lineup. George Scott and Jim Lonborg blossomed. And Carl Yastrzemski, who had his finest year, won the Triple Crown.

Baseball is a funny game. Joe Garagiola would vouch for that statement. So would John McGraw, Connie Mack, Joe Cronin, Walt Alston, Ralph Houk, and Dick Williams!

Casey in New York

"Casey in New York." That could be the title of a song. If it were, it would be strictly biographical. For Casey Stengel, one of the most colorful characters in the history of baseball, was the only player and manager who has been directly connected with all four of the New York franchises: the Dodgers, the Giants, the Yankees, and the Mets.

"The Old Professor" played the first six years of his 14-year career with the Dodgers. Twice during that span he hit .316 in a season. After two years with the Pirates and one and a half years with the Phillies, he moved to the Giants, with whom he hit .368 and .339 during a two and a half year tenure among the denizens of Coogan's Bluff. In the 1923 World Series he hit two home runs that made the difference in the Giants' only victories over their arch rivals, the Yankees.

Managerial-wise, Stengel guided the Dodgers from 1934 to 1936, with his best finish being a fifth-place effort in 1935. After a six-year stint with the Braves (1938-43), he next got the chance to manage a major league team when the Yankees named him the successor to Bucky Harris in 1949.

Stengel made the most of his opportunity. He and his players reeled off five consecutive world championships, a major league record. In 1954, when the Yankees' streak came to an end, he called the shots in 103 wins, a personal high; but the Indians won 111 games, the all-time high in the American League. Stengel's team bounced back to win four consecutive pennants from 1955 to 1958. Had the Indians not had that sensational year in 1954, the Yankees would have won ten consecutive pennants under Stengel's direction. That's a pretty good record for a manager who never led a National League team to a first-division finish in 13 years at the helm.

When the Yankees lost the 1960 World Series to the Pirates in seven games, the Pinstripers' brass decided that Stengel was too old to lead the Bronx Bombers. So Casey moved his managerial act to Long Island, where he directed the expansion team Mets to four tenth-place finishes. The Mets of those years were most probably the sorriest excuse for a team in the history of major league baseball. But they laid the groundwork for championship clubs in 1969 and 1973.

The 1969 Mets were called "Destiny's Darlings." Short on talent, they were big on desire. They had a certain charisma that was difficult to define. It was very much like that of their leader and guiding force—Casey Stengel!

Leo and New York

Leo Durocher was another player and manager who had a love-hate relationship with New York.

"The Lip" broke into the majors with the Yankees in 1925. After stays with the Reds and Cardinals, with whom he short-stopped the "Gas House Gang" to the 1934 World Series championship, he moved to Brooklyn, where in 1939 he became the playing-manager of the Dodgers. During his nine-year rule the Dodgers won one pennant and lost another (in 1946) in a play-off series against the Cardinals.

Approximately half way through the 1948 season, Durocher was released by the Dodgers and signed by the Giants, the "Bums" archenemy. In eight years with the men from Coogan's Bluff, Durocher won two pennants and one World Series. Twice during that time, he edged the Dodgers out for first place. Once he finished second to the Dodgers.

He never worked for the New York Mets' organization. But in 1969 he got as close to "The Amazin' Ones" as he wanted to get. Manager of Chicago at the time, he kept the Cubs in first place for most of the season. But the Bruins faded in the stretch, and the Mets finished fast to win the pennant by eight games.

No stranger to fate, Durocher had to step aside and make way for "Destiny's Darlings!"

Captain Hook

In an era when managers Dick Williams, Alvin Dark, and Sparky "Captain Hook" Anderson have made names for themselves by going to the bull pen whenever one of their starters gets himself into trouble, it might be surprising to learn that there was once a time when managers had complete game faith in their starters.

In 1956, for example, the Dodgers defeated the Yankees in the first two games. But the Yankees, on the strength of five straight complete games, bounced back to win the Series, four games to three. The five Yankees' pitchers who threw the complete games were Whitey Ford, Tom Sturdivant, Don Larsen, Bob Turley, and Johnny Kucks.

The last three games of the Series ended in shutouts. In game five Don Larsen "perfect-gamed" Sal Maglie, 2-0; in game six Clem Labine outlasted Bob Turley in ten innings, 1-0; and in game seven Johnny Kucks blanked Don Newcombe, 9-0.

By way of contrast, Mike Torrez of the 1977 Yankees pitched the first complete game victory (in the third game) for a winning world title team since Steve Blass of the Pirates turned the trick in the final game of the 1971 World Series.

In between, the championship teams sent 32 consecutive starters to the mound without getting a complete game!

Mack and Finley: The Same Fate?

Will the Oakland A's, who have had their team decimated by diamondmen who have played out their options, find out that history is going to repeat itself? Will they suffer the same fate as their ancestors, the Philadelphia Athletics, who lost their great stars after building dynasties in the 1910s and 1930s?

The Athletics from 1910-14 won four pennants and three World Series. But when they got swept by the "Miracle Braves" in 1914, owner-manager Connie Mack over-reacted: he got rid of the nucleus of his franchise. Eddie Plank and Chief Bender jumped to the Federal League, Eddie Collins and Ed Murphy went to the White Sox, Jack Coombs didn't make the team, Bob Shawkey and Home Run Baker moved to New York, and Jack Barry and Herb Pennock wound up with the Red Sox. The upshoot of Mack's housecleaning was that the Athletics finished last for seven straight years. Mack, who had reacted on impulse, resigned himself to repent in leisure.

In time, however, he rebuilt the franchise; and the A's won three pennants and two World Series from 1929-31. But Mack had not learned his lesson. When the Cardinals upset the A's in the 1931 World Series, he began to unload his star players once more. He sent Al Simmons, Jimmy Dykes, and Mule Haas to the White Sox; he shipped Jimmy Foxx and Lefty Grove to the Red Sox; and he dispatched Mickey Cochrane to the Tigers. By 1935 the demolition derby was completed; and the A's toppled from the sublime to the ridiculous again. They finished last in nine of the following 12 years. And they did not recover. Mack managed only one A's team that finished in the first division from 1934 to 1950, the year that he retired.

Under Charlie Finley, however, the A's once again rebuilt themselves. They reeled off consecutive world titles in 1972, 1973, and 1974. But this time the players have rebelled. Many of them have played out their options and happily moved on to other franchises. Gone are Catfish Hunter, Ken Holtzman, Reggie Jackson, Bert Campaneris, Joe Rudi, Sal Bando, and Gene Tenace.

Finley says that he can win without them. But somewhere a sage old spirit named Connic Mack must be sadly shaking his head. For Finley is used to outplaying contemporary teams in the American League. This time he is up against history.

And history has a tendency to repeat itself. For example, the A's finished sixth in their division in 1977!

Murderers' Row

The Yankees have compiled the most incredible World Series record in the history of the game.

Overall, they have won 31 pennants and 21 World Series. They lost their first two World Series (1921 and 1922) and three of their last four post-season get-togethers (1963, 1964, and 1976). In between, they won 20 of 25, and once again in 1977.

During one stretch (1927, 1928, and 1932) they won 12 consecutive World Series games; during another stretch (1937, 1938, 1939, and 1941) they won ten.

The Expo Express

The Montreal Expos have yet to play in a World Series. But many of their one-time stars have played in at least one.

Mike Marshall, for example. (He played with Los Angeles, against Oakland in 1974). Don Clendennon, Rusty Staub, and Mike Torrez are three others. All played in a World Series while they were members of a New York team.

Clendennon, shipped to the Mets in 1969, helped "The Amazin' Ones" win the pennant in that year and then smashed three home runs in the World Series while New York upset Baltimore in five games.

Staub, traded in a deal for Ken Singleton, also helped the Mets win a pennant, this time in 1973. In New York's World Series loss to Oakland, "La Grande Orange" hit a torrid .423.

Torrez, sent to Baltimore in 1975, won 20 games with the Orioles. In the following two years, he posted 16 victories for the A's and 17 triumphs for the Yankees. In addition, he won two games, including the wrap-up one, without a defeat in the 1977 World Series.

Ken Singleton, who also played for a New York team (the Mets) and Montreal, has never played in a World Series. But he's probably the best player the Expos have given away for the least exchange. In 1975 he, along with Torrez, were peddled to the Orioles for Dave McNally, Bill Kirkpatrick, and Rich Coggins. None of the three new additions made a significant contribution to the Montreal ball club.

A .284 hitter in his three years with the Expos, Singleton enjoyed his best year in Montreal in 1973 when he batted .302, banged 23 home runs, and drove home 103 RBI, the team's all-time high.

His batting average in three years with the Orioles is .302. In 1977, at the prime age of 30, he batted .327, belted 23 homers, and drove home 97 runs.

With statistics like these he's bound to wind up in a World Series one of these years. But not in Montreal!

Blue (Chip) Jays

The Toronto Blue Jays didn't end up on top of the standings in their first year as a major league franchise, but two of their players performed well enough to end up in the all-time record books: Bob Bailor and Dave Lemanczyk.

Bailor, who batted .310 with five home runs and 32 RBI, turned in the highest average in history for a player (on a first-year expansion team) who qualified for the batting title. (A player needs 502 official plate appearances to do so.)

Some previous players, on first-year expansion teams, who hit better than .300 were Gene Woodling, who batted .313 for the Senators in 1961; Richie Ashburn, who stroked .306 for the Mets in 1962; and Rusty Staub, who banged .302 for the Expos in 1969. Only Staub had enough plate appearances to qualify for the batting title, though.

Roy Howell of the Blue Jays, who did not have the official number of at-bats to qualify, matched Staub's average by hitting .302 in 1977.

Lemanczyk, who equalled a feat that had been performed only once before, won 13 games in 1977. His overall record was 13 wins, 16 losses, and 4.29 ERA.

The only other pitcher on a first-year expansion team who has won as many as 13 games was Gene Brabender, who turned in a 13-14 record for the Seattle Pilots in 1969.

INDEX